JACQUES DERRIDA

D0544310

'Excellent, strong, clear and original'. *Jacques Derrida*.

'A strong, inventive and daring book that does much more than most introductions are capable of even dreaming'. *Diane Elam, Cardiff University*.

'Readers couldn't ask for a more authoritative and knowledgeable guide. Although there is no playing down of the immensity of the implications of Derrida's work, Royle's direct and often funny mode of address will make it less threatening than it can often appear to beginners'. *Derek Attridge, University of York*.

In this entertaining and provocative introduction, Royle offers lucid explanations of various key ideas, including deconstruction, differance and the democracy to come. He also gives attention, however, to a range of perhaps less obvious topics, such as earthquakes, animals and animality, ghosts, monstrosity, the poematic, drugs, gifts, secrets, war and mourning. Derrida is seen as an extraordinarily inventive thinker, as well as a brilliantly imaginative and often very funny writer. Other critical introductions tend to highlight the specifically philosophical nature and genealogy of his work. Royle's book proceeds in a new and different way, in particular by focusing on the crucial but strange place of literature in Derrida's writings. He thus provides an appreciation and understanding based on detailed reference to Derrida's texts, interwoven with close readings of literary works. In doing so, he explores Derrida's consistent view that deconstruction is a 'coming-to-terms with literature'. He emphasizes the ways in which 'literature', for Derrida, is indissociably bound up with other concerns, such as philosophy and psychoanalysis, politics and ethics, responsibility and justice, law and democracy.

Nicholas Royle is Professor of English at the University of Sussex. His books include *Telepathy and Literature: Essays on the Reading Mind* (1990), *After Derrida* (1995), *The Uncanny* (2003) and (with Andrew Bennett) *An Introduction to Literature, Criticism and Theory* (1999). He is also the editor of *Deconstructions: A User's Guide* (2000).

ROUTLEDGE CRITICAL THINKERS

Series Editor: Robert Eaglestone, Royal Holloway, University of London

Routledge Critical Thinkers is a series of accessible introductions to key figures in contemporary critical thought.

With a unique focus on historical and intellectual contexts, each volume examines a key theorist's:

* significance
* motivation
* key ideas and their sources
* impact on other thinkers

Concluding with extensively annotated guides to further reading, *Routledge Critical Thinkers* are the student's passport to today's most exciting critical thought.

For further details on this series, see www.literature.routledge.com/rct

JACQUES DERRIDA

Nicholas Royle

Routledge
Taylor & Francis Group

LONDON AND NEW YORK

First published 2003
by Routledge
2 Park Square, Milton Park, Abingdon, Oxon, OX14 4RN

Simultaneously published in the USA and Canada
by Routledge
270 Madison Ave, New York, NY 10016

Reprinted 2004 (twice), 2006, 2008 (twice)

Routledge is an imprint of the Taylor & Francis Group, an informa business

Typeset in Perpetua by Florence Production Ltd, Stoodleigh, Devon
Printed and bound in Great Britain by
TJ International Ltd, Padstow, Cornwall

British Library Cataloguing in Publication Data
A catalogue record for this book is available from the British Library

Library of Congress Cataloging in Publication Data
  Royle, Nicholas, 1957–
    Jacques Derrida / Nicholas Royle.
      p. cm – (Routledge critical thinkers)
    Includes bibliographical references and index.
    1. Derrida, Jacques. I. Title. II. Series.
    B2430.D484 R69 2003
    194–dc21

                                                    2002151055

ISBN10: 0–415–22930–8 (hbk)
ISBN10: 0–415–22931–6 (pbk)

ISBN13: 978–0–415–22930–2 (hbk)
ISBN13: 978–0–415–22931–9 (pbk)

CONTENTS

SERIES EDITOR'S PREFACE

The books in this series offer introductions to major critical thinkers who have influenced literary studies and the humanities. The *Routledge Critical Thinkers* series provides the books you can turn to first when a new name or concept appears in your studies.

Each book will equip you to approach a key thinker's original texts by explaining her or his key ideas, putting them into context and, perhaps most importantly, showing you why this thinker is considered to be significant. The emphasis is on concise, clearly written guides which do not presuppose a specialist knowledge. Although the focus is on particular figures, the series stresses that no critical thinker ever existed in a vacuum but, instead, emerged from a broader intellectual, cultural and social history. Finally, these books will act as a bridge between you and the thinker's original texts: not replacing them but rather complementing what she or he wrote.

These books are necessary for a number of reasons. In his 1997 autobiography, *Not Entitled*, the literary critic Frank Kermode wrote of a time in the 1960s:

> On beautiful summer lawns, young people lay together all night, recovering from their daytime exertions and listening to a troupe of Balinese musicians. Under their blankets or their sleeping bags, they would chat drowsily about the gurus of the time. ... What they repeated was largely hearsay; hence my

lunchtime suggestion, quite impromptu, for a series of short, very cheap books offering authoritative but intelligible introductions to such figures.

There is still a need for 'authoritative and intelligible introductions'. But this series reflects a different world from the 1960s. New thinkers have emerged and the reputations of others have risen and fallen, as new research has developed. New methodologies and challenging ideas have spread through arts and humanities. The study of literature is no longer – if it ever was – simply the study and evaluation of poems, novels and plays. It is also the study of ideas, issues and difficulties which arise in any literary text and in its interpretation. Other arts and humanities subjects have changed in analogous ways.

With these changes, new problems have emerged. The ideas and issues behind these radical changes in the humanities are often presented without reference to wider contexts or as theories which you can simply 'add on' to the texts you read. Certainly, there's nothing wrong with picking out selected ideas or using what comes to hand – indeed, some thinkers have argued that this is, in fact, all we can do. However, it is sometimes forgotten that each new idea comes from the pattern and development of somebody's thought and it is important to study the range and context of their ideas. Against theories 'floating in space', the *Routledge Critical Thinkers* series places key thinkers and their ideas firmly back in their contexts.

More than this, these books reflect the need to go back to the thinker's own texts and ideas. Every interpretation of an idea, even the most seemingly innocent one, offers its own 'spin', implicitly or explicitly. To read only books on a thinker, rather than texts by that thinker, is to deny yourself a chance of making up your own mind. Sometimes what makes a significant figure's work hard to approach is not so much its style or content as the feeling of not knowing where to start. The purpose of these books is to give you a 'way in' by offering an accessible overview of these thinkers' ideas and works and by guiding your further reading, starting with each thinker's own texts. To use a metaphor from the philosopher Ludwig Wittgenstein (1889–1951), these books are ladders, to be thrown away after you have climbed to the next level. Not only, then, do they equip you to approach new ideas, but also they empower you, by leading you back to the theorist's own texts and encouraging you to develop your own informed opinions.

Finally, these books are necessary because, just as intellectual needs have changed, the education systems around the world – the contexts in which introductory books are usually read – have changed radically, too. What was suitable for the minority higher education system of the 1960s is not suitable for the larger, wider, more diverse, high technology education systems of the twenty-first century. These changes call not just for new, up-to-date, introductions but new methods of presentation. The presentational aspects of *Routledge Critical Thinkers* have been developed with today's students in mind.

Each book in the series has a similar structure. They begin with a section offering an overview of the life and ideas of each thinker and explain why she or he is important. The central section of each book discusses the thinker's key ideas, their context, evolution and reception. Each book concludes with a survey of the thinker's impact, outlining how their ideas have been taken up and developed by others. In addition, there is a detailed final section suggesting and describing books for further reading. This is not a 'tacked-on' section but an integral part of each volume. In the first part of this section you will find brief descriptions of the thinker's key works, then, following this, information on the most useful critical works and, in some cases, on relevant websites. This section will guide you in your reading, enabling you to follow your interests and develop your own projects. Throughout each book, references are given in what is known as the Harvard system (the author and the date of a work cited are given in the text and you can look up the full details in the bibliography at the back). This offers a lot of information in very little space. The books also explain technical terms and use boxes to describe events or ideas in more detail, away from the main emphasis of the discussion. Boxes are also used at times to highlight definitions of terms frequently used or coined by a thinker. In this way, the boxes serve as a kind of glossary, easily identified when flicking through the book.

The thinkers in the series are 'critical' for three reasons. First, they are examined in the light of subjects which involve criticism: principally literary studies or English and cultural studies, but also other disciplines which rely on the criticism of books, ideas, theories and unquestioned assumptions. Second, they are critical because studying their work will provide you with a 'tool kit' for your own informed critical reading and thought, which will make you critical. Third, these thinkers are critical because they are crucially important: they deal with ideas and questions which can overturn conventional understandings of the world, of texts, of everything we take for granted, leaving us with a deeper understanding of what we already knew and with new ideas.

No introduction can tell you everything. However, by offering a way into critical thinking, this series hopes to begin to engage you in an activity which is productive, constructive and potentially life-changing.

ACKNOWLEDGEMENTS

For their many helpful and constructive comments I would like to thank my indefatigably good-humoured and supportive editor Bob Eaglestone, Liz Thompson at Routledge and the anonymous authors of the four readers' reports on the original typescript of this work. Much of the material in this book was initially presented as a series of lectures at the University of Sussex in the autumn of 2001. I would like to express my gratitude and indebtedness to those who were there: Richard Adburgham, Jana Beyreuther, Stephen Cowburn, Gary Groves, Jude Hunton, Paul James, Michael Jonik, Jinan Joudeh, Abigail Maxwell, Christopher Piper, Katherina Pottakis, Maria Sanengen, Mark Sheerin, David O'Connor Thompson and Say Fern Toh. I have made some attempt to erase traces of 'original oral delivery', but not too much, I hope.

ABBREVIATIONS

TEXTS BY DERRIDA

Note: where possible (for example, Che, DTB, FL, and S) I refer to English translations that have appeared in bilingual editions, i.e. the version most conveniently enabling the reader to consult the French text as well as English translation. All references to the original French elsewhere (for instance when in the interests of clarity I have slightly modified the English versions) are to the standard French editions of the text in question.

A   *Aporias: Dying – Awaiting (One Another at) the 'Limits of Truth'*, trans. Thomas Dutoit (Stanford: Stanford University Press, 1993).

AC   'Aphorism Countertime', trans. Nicholas Royle, in *Acts of Literature*, ed. Derek Attridge (London and New York: Routledge, 1992), 414–33.

Ad   *Adieu, to Emmanuel Levinas*, trans. Pascale-Anne Brault and Michael Naas (Stanford: Stanford University Press, 1999).

AF   *Archive Fever: A Freudian Impression*, trans. Eric Prenowitz (Chicago: Chicago University Press, 1996).

AFRC   *The Archeology of the Frivolous: Reading Condillac*, trans. John P. Leavey, Jr (Pittsburgh: Duquesne University Press, 1980).

      Deconstruction and Criticism (New York: Seabury Press, 1979), 75–176. (Extracts in DRBB.)

C   'Circumfession', in *Jacques Derrida*, trans. Geoffrey Bennington (Chicago: Chicago University Press, 1993).

Che   'Che cos'è la poesia?', trans. Peggy Kamuf, in *A Derrida Reader: Between the Blinds*, ed. Kamuf (London and New York: Harvester, 1991), 221–37. (Also published in *P.*)

CHM   'Cogito and the History of Madness', in *Writing and Difference*, trans. Alan Bass (London: Routledge and Kegan Paul, 1978), 31–63.

Cho   'Choreographies', trans. Christie V. McDonald, in *Points . . . Interviews, 1974–94*, ed. Elisabeth Weber (Stanford: Stanford University Press, 1995), 89–108.

D   *Dissemination*, trans. Barbara Johnson (Chicago: Chicago University Press, 1981).

DA   'The Deconstruction of Actuality: An Interview with Jacques Derrida', trans. Jonathan Rée, in Martin McQuillan, ed., *Deconstruction: A Reader* (Edinburgh: Edinburgh University Press, 2000), 527–53. (Also in ET and N.)

Dec   'Deconstruction in America: An Interview with Jacques Derrida', trans. James Creech, *Critical Exchange*, 17 (1985): 1–33.

Dem   'Demeure: Fiction and Testimony' (with Maurice Blanchot's *The Instant of My Death*), trans. Elizabeth Rottenberg (Stanford: Stanford University Press, 2000).

DI   'Declarations of Independence', trans. Tom Keenan and Tom Pepper, *New Political Science*, 15 (1986): 7–15. (Also in N.)

Dia   'Dialanguages', trans. Peggy Kamuf, in *Points . . . Interviews, 1974–94*, ed. Elisabeth Weber (Stanford: Stanford University Press, 1995), 132–55.

Diff   'Différance', in *Margins of Philosophy*, trans. Alan Bass (Chicago: Chicago University Press, 1982), 1–27. (Also in SP; extracts in DRBB.)

Diss   'Dissemination', in *Dissemination*, trans. Barbara Johnson (Chicago: Chicago University Press, 1981), 287–366.

DO   'Deconstruction and the Other', Interview with Richard Kearney, in Kearney, *Dialogues with Contemporary Continental Thinkers* (Manchester: Manchester University Press, 1984), 105–26.

FS   'Force and Signification', in *Writing and Difference*, trans. Alan
          Bass (London: Routledge and Kegan Paul, 1978), 3–30.
FSW   'Freud and the Scene of Writing', in *Writing and Difference*,
          trans. Alan Bass (London: Routledge and Kegan Paul, 1978),
          196–231.
FV   'Le facteur de la vérité', in *The Post Card: From Socrates to Freud
          and Beyond*, trans. Alan Bass (Chicago: Chicago University
          Press, 1987), 411–96. (Extracts in DRBB.)
G   *Glas*, trans. John P. Leavey, Jr, and Richard Rand (London:
          University of Nebraska Press, 1986). (Extracts in DRBB.)
GARW   'Geopsychoanalysis: ". . . and the Rest of the World"', trans.
          Donald Nicholson-Smith, in *American Imago*, vol. 48, no. 2
          (1991): 199–231.
GD   *The Gift of Death*, trans. David Wills (Chicago: Chicago
          University Press, 1995).
GT   *Given Time: 1. Counterfeit Money*, trans. Peggy Kamuf (Chicago:
          Chicago University Press, 1992).
H   'How to Avoid Speaking: Denials', trans. Ken Frieden, in
          Derrida and Negative Theology, eds Harold Coward and Toby
          Foshay (Albany: State University of New York Press, 1992),
          73–142.
Hos   *Of Hospitality: Anne Dufourmantelle Invites Jacques Derrida to
          Respond*, trans. Rachel Bowlby (Stanford: Stanford University
          Press, 2000).
HPH   'Heidegger, the Philosophers' Hell', trans. Peggy Kamuf, in
          Points. . . Interviews, 1974–94, ed. Elisabeth Weber (Stanford:
          Stanford University Press, 1995), 181–90.
Ist   '*Istrice 2: Ick bünn all hier*', trans. Peggy Kamuf, in *Points . . .
          Interviews, 1974–94*, ed. Elisabeth Weber (Stanford: Stanford
          University Press, 1995), 300–26.
Ja   '*Ja*, or the *faux-bond* II', trans. Peggy Kamuf, in *Points . . .
          Interviews, 1974–94*, ed. Elisabeth Weber (Stanford: Stanford
          University Press, 1995), 30–77.
LG   'The Law of Genre', trans. Avital Ronell, in *Acts of Literature*,
          ed. Derek Attridge (London and New York: Routledge,
          1992), 221–52.
LI   'Limited Inc a b c . . .', trans. Samuel Weber, in *Limited Inc*
          (Evanston, Illinois: Northwestern University Press, 1988),
          29–110.

O   'Outwork', in *Dissemination*, trans. Barbara Johnson (Chicago: Chicago University Press, 1981), 3–59.

O&G   '*Ousia* and *Grammē*: Note on a Note from *Being and Time*', in *Margins of Philosophy*, trans. Alan Bass (Chicago: Chicago University Press, 1982), 29–67.

OCF   *On Cosmopolitanism and Forgiveness*, trans. Mark Dooley and Michael Hughes (London: Routledge, 2001).

OG   *Of Grammatology*, trans. Gayatri Chakravorty Spivak (Baltimore: Johns Hopkins University Press, 1976). (Extracts in AL and DRBB.)

OGI   *Edmund Husserl's 'Origin of Geometry': An Introduction*, trans. John P. Leavey, Jr (Stony Brook, New York: Nicolas Hays, 1978).

OH   *The Other Heading: Reflections on Today's Europe*, trans. Pascale-Anne Brault and Michael B. Naas (Bloomington: Indiana University Press, 1992).

ON   *On the Name*, ed. Thomas Dutoit, trans. David Wood, John P. Leavey, Jr and Ian McLeod (Stanford: Stanford University Press, 1995).

OS   *Of Spirit: Heidegger and the Question*, trans. Geoffrey Bennington and Rachel Bowlby (Chicago: Chicago University Press, 1989).

P   *Points . . . Interviews, 1974–94*, ed. Elisabeth Weber, trans. Peggy Kamuf and others (Stanford: Stanford University Press, 1995).

PF   *Politics of Friendship*, trans. George Collins (London and New York: Verso, 1997).

PIO   'Psyche: Inventions of the Other', trans. Catherine Porter, in *Reading de Man Reading*, eds Lindsay Waters and Wlad Godzich (Minneapolis: University of Minnesota Press, 1989), 25–65. (Extracts in AL and DRBB.)

POO   'Passions: "An Oblique Offering"', trans. David Wood, in *Derrida: A Critical Reader*, ed. David Wood (Oxford and Cambridge, MA: Basil Blackwell, 1992), 5–35. (Also published in ON.)

Pos   *Positions*, trans. Alan Bass (Chicago: Chicago University Press, 1981).

PP   'Plato's Pharmacy', in *Dissemination*, trans. Barbara Johnson (Chicago: Chicago University Press, 1981), 63–171. (Extracts in DRBB.)

PR   'The Principle of Reason: The University in the Eyes of Its Pupils', trans. Catherine Porter and Edward P. Morris, *Diacritics* 13: 3 (1983): 3–20.

Pro   'Proverb: "He That Would Pun . . ."', Foreword to *Glassary* (Lincoln: Nebraska University Press, 1986), 17–20.

PS   'Psychoanalysis Searches the States of Its Soul: The Impossible Beyond of a Sovereign Cruelty', in *Without Alibi*, ed., trans. and with an Introduction by Peggy Kamuf (Stanford: Stanford University Press, 2002), 238–80.

PTP   'Passages – from Traumatism to Promise', trans. Peggy Kamuf, in *Points . . . Interviews, 1974–94*, ed. Elisabeth Weber (Stanford: Stanford University Press, 1995), 372–95.

QQ   'Qual Quelle: Valéry's Sources', in *Margins of Philosophy*, trans. Alan Bass (Chicago: Chicago University Press, 1982), 273–306.

RD   'The Rhetoric of Drugs', trans. Michael Israel, in *Points . . . Interviews, 1974–94*, ed. Elisabeth Weber, trans. Peggy Kamuf and others (Stanford: Stanford University Press, 1995), 228–54.

RDP   'Remarks on Deconstruction and Pragmatism', trans. Simon Critchley, in *Deconstruction and Pragmatism*, ed. Chantal Mouffe (London and New York: Routledge, 1996), 77–88.

RI   *Right of Inspection*, trans. David Wills, with photographs by Marie-Françoise Plissart (New York: Monacelli Press, 1998). No page numbers.

RLW   'Racism's Last Word', trans. Peggy Kamuf, *Critical Inquiry* 12: 1 (1985): 290–9.

RP   *Resistances of Psychoanalysis*, trans. Peggy Kamuf, Pascale-Anne Brault and Michael Naas (Stanford: Stanford University Press, 1998).

S   *Signéponge / Signsponge*, trans. Richard Rand (New York: Columbia University Press, 1984). (Extracts of this text are also included in *AL*.)

SEC   'Signature Event Context', trans. Samuel Weber and Jeffrey Mehlman, in *Limited Inc* (Evanston, Illinois: Northwestern University Press, 1988), 1–23. (Also in DRBB.)

SF   'To Speculate – on "Freud"', in *The Post Card: From Socrates to Freud and Beyond*, trans. Alan Bass (Chicago: Chicago University Press, 1987), 257–409. (Extracts in DRBB.)

Sh   'Shibboleth', trans. Joshua Wilner, in *Midrash and Literature*,
          eds Geoffrey H. Hartman and Sanford Budick (New Haven:
          Yale University Press, 1986), 307–47. (Extracts in AL.)

SM   *Specters of Marx: The State of the Debt, the Work of Mourning, and
          the New International*, trans. Peggy Kamuf (London and New
          York: Routledge, 1994).

SN   'Sauf le nom', trans. John P. Leavey, Jr, in *On the Name*, ed.
          Thomas Dutoit, trans. David Wood, John P. Leavey, Jr and Ian
          McLeod (Stanford: Stanford University Press, 1995), 33–85.

SOO   'A Silkworm of One's Own', trans. Geoffrey Bennington, in
          Derridas, special issue of the *Oxford Literary Review*, vol. 18
          (1997): 3–65. (Also in AR.)

SP   *Speech and Phenomena and Other Essays on Husserl's Theory of
          Signs*, trans. David Allison (Evanston, Illinois: Northwestern
          University Press, 1973). (Extracts in DRBB.)

Sp   *Spurs: Nietzsche's Styles / Eperons: Les Styles de Nietzsche*, trans.
          Barbara Harlow (Chicago: University of Chicago Press,
          1979). (Extracts in DRBB.)

SSP   'Structure, Sign, and Play in the Discourse of the Human
          Sciences', in *Writing and Difference*, trans. Alan Bass (London:
          Routledge and Kegan Paul, 1978), 278–93.

SST   'Some Statements and Truisms About Neo-Logisms, New-
          isms, Postisms, Parasitisms, and Other Small Seismisms',
          trans. Anne Tomiche, in *The States of 'Theory': History, Art and
          Critical Discourse*, ed. David Carroll (New York: Columbia
          University Press, 1990), 63–95.

T   'Telepathy', trans. Nicholas Royle, in Martin McQuillan,
          ed., *Deconstruction: A Reader* (Edinburgh: Edinburgh Univer-
          sity Press, 2000), 496–526.

TC   'The Theater of Cruelty and the Closure of Representation',
          in *Writing and Difference*, trans. Alan Bass (London: Routledge
          and Kegan Paul, 1978), 232–50.

TNOF   'This Is Not An Oral Footnote', in *Annotation and Its Texts*,
          ed. Stephen A. Barney (Oxford: Oxford University Press,
          1991), 192–205.

TNON   ' "There Is No *One* Narcissism" (Autobiophotographies)',
          trans. Peggy Kamuf, in *Points . . . Interviews, 1974–94*, ed.
          Elisabeth Weber (Stanford: Stanford University Press, 1995),
          196–215.

TOJ   'The Time is Out of Joint', trans. Peggy Kamuf, in *Deconstruction is/in America: A New Sense of the Political*, ed. Anselm Haverkamp (New York: New York University Press, 1995), 14–38.

TP   *The Truth in Painting*, trans. Geoff Bennington and Ian McLeod (Chicago: University of Chicago Press, 1987). (Extracts in DRBB.)

TS   'I Have a Taste for the Secret', Jacques Derrida in conversation with Maurizio Ferraris and Giorgio Vattimo, in Derrida and Ferraris, *A Taste for the Secret*, trans. Giacomo Donis (Cambridge, UK: Polity, 2001), 3–92.

TSICL   'This Strange Institution Called Literature', trans. Geoffrey Bennington and Rachel Bowlby, in *Acts of Literature*, ed. Derek Attridge (London and New York: Routledge, 1992), 33–75.

TTBS   'Title (to be specified)', trans. Tom Conley, *SubStance*, 31 (1981): 5–22.

TTP   'The Time of a Thesis: Punctuations', trans. Kathleen McLaughlin, in *Philosophy in France Today*, ed. Alan Montefiore (Cambridge: Cambridge University Press, 1983), 34–50.

TWJ   'Two Words for Joyce', trans. Geoff Bennington, in *Post-Structuralist Joyce: Essays from the French*, eds Derek Attridge and Daniel Ferrer (Cambridge: Cambridge University Press, 1984), 145–59.

U   'Unsealing ("The Old New Language")', trans. Peggy Kamuf, in *Points . . . Interviews, 1974–94*, ed. Elisabeth Weber (Stanford: Stanford University Press, 1995), 115–31.

UG   'Ulysses Gramophone: Hear Say Yes in Joyce', trans. Tina Kendall and Shari Benstock in *Acts of Literature*, ed. Derek Attridge (London and New York: Routledge, 1992), 256–309. (Extracts in DRBB.)

US   'To Unsense the Subjectile', trans. Mary Ann Caws, in Jacques Derrida and Paule Thévenin, *The Secret Art of Antonin Artaud* (London and Cambridge, MA: MIT Press, 1998), 59–157.

UWC   'The University Without Condition', in *Without Alibi*, ed., trans. and with an Introduction by Peggy Kamuf (Stanford: Stanford University Press, 2002). (Also in Cohen 2001.)

V   'Voice II', trans. Verena Andermatt Conley, in *Points . . . Interviews, 1974–94*, ed. Elisabeth Weber (Stanford: Stanford University Press, 1995), 156–70.

VR   'The Villanova Roundtable: A Conversation with Jacques Derrida', in *Deconstruction in a Nutshell*, ed. John D. Caputo (New York: Fordham University Press, 1997), 3–28.

WA   *Without Alibi*, ed., trans. and with an Introduction by Peggy Kamuf (Stanford: Stanford University Press, 2002).

WAP   *Who's Afraid of Philosophy: Right to Philosophy 1*, trans. Jan Plug (Stanford: Stanford University Press, 2002).

WB   'Women in the Beehive: A Seminar with Jacques Derrida', in *Men in Feminism*, ed. Alice Jardine and Paul Smith (London and New York: Methuen, 1987), 189–203.

WD   *Writing and Difference*, trans. Alan Bass (London: Routledge and Kegan Paul, 1978).

WIP   'The Work of Intellectuals and the Press (The Bad Example: How the *New York Review of Books* and Company Do Business)', trans. Peggy Kamuf, in *Points . . . Interviews, 1974–94*, ed. Elisabeth Weber (Stanford: Stanford University Press, 1995), 422–54, 482–7.

WM   'White Mythology: Metaphor in the Text of Philosophy', in *Margins of Philosophy*, trans. Alan Bass (Chicago: Chicago University Press, 1982), 207–71.

WoM   *The Work of Mourning*, ed. Pascale-Anne Brault and Michael Naas (Chicago: Chicago University Press, 2001).

WHY DERRIDA?

Why Derrida? In accordance with the 'similar structure' (p. ix) of each book in this series, *Routledge Critical Thinkers*, I must begin by trying to respond to this question – with luck in ways that will interest and even amuse you (since the question, I confess, is not one that I am able to take altogether seriously, for reasons that I hope will become clear). No doubt there will have been some minimal understanding already presupposed here: 'Derrida' is not the name of some new high-energy drink or a prospective location for the next Olympic Games. 'Why Derrida?': I have just put the question in quotation marks, but in effect it already was, from the beginning. Here, then, is my first 'proper Derrida quote'. He says: 'Be alert to these invisible quotation marks, even within a word' (LO 76). 'Why Derrida?' How much understanding can or should be assumed in relation to this question?

Let us consider the following, seemingly innocuous formulation:

'Derrida' is the name of a man, a Jewish Algerian-French philosopher, born in 1930.

To borrow a phrase from one of his more extraordinary recent essays: 'One could spend years on this sentence' (Dem 54). The sentence raises a number of questions that are crucial to Derrida's work. For example:

1   What is happening when someone's name is put in quotation marks? What are quotation marks? Where do they begin? What are

the limits of 'quotability'? How do we decide what should or should not be in quotation marks? Derrida's work, as we will see, is about '[putting] into practice a vigilant but . . . general *use* of quotation marks' (SST 77). Exploring the sense that 'it is no longer possible to *use* seriously the words of tradition', his work is concerned with 'destabiliz[ing] . . . the opposition between discourse *with* and discourse *without* quotation marks', in other words with destabilizing 'philosophy in its entirety, theory in its entirety' (SST 74–5).

2   What indeed is a name? What relation does it have to its bearer? Is one's name one's own? Is a proper name ever truly proper? Derrida will insist, for example, on the logic according to which one is in some sense always 'a stranger to [one's] name': see AC 427. As he has said of the name 'Derrida': 'I love this name [Derrida], which is not mine of course (the only possibility of loving a name is that it not be yours)' (AI 219).

3   What is a man, as opposed to a woman, say, or as distinct from an animal or a machine? Derrida complicates all such oppositions or distinctions. He is concerned, for example, with 'sexual differences in the plural' (V 163), with a thinking that goes 'beyond the opposition feminine/masculine, beyond bisexuality as well, beyond homosexuality and heterosexuality which come to the same thing' (Cho 108). Derrida is concerned with a critical thinking that begins with a troubling of any straightforward distinctions between the human and the animal. Having remarked that '[n]o one can deny the suffering, fear or panic, the terror or fright that humans witness in certain animals', he concludes: 'The animal looks at us, and we are naked before it. Thinking perhaps begins there' (ATA 397). At the same time, he is concerned with a new thinking of the machine, construing intimate links between the machine, repetition, writing and death. He suggests that there is no writing and no memory without mechanical repetition: the machine is death, he says, 'the origin of machines is the relation to death' (FSW 227).

4   What does 'Jewish' mean? What is implied, what is at stake when someone is identified in terms of his Hebrew descent or religion? Imagine if 'Christian' were applied in the same way, to every relevant writer or other so-called public figure you might care to consider. Derrida has said that he is and is not Jewish, that he is and is not Christian. How does religion play a part in questions of

identity? How do we deal with a thinker whose concern is with what 'blocks every relationship to theology' (Pos 40), a thinker impelled by what he has called 'a messianism without religion' (SM 59)?

5 'Algerian-French': what does it mean for someone to be identified in terms of coming from or belonging to more than one country, especially countries with as twisted a history, producing such a 'disorder of identity' (MO 14), as Algeria and France?

6 What is a 'philosopher'? What is going on when someone is described as such? What happens when it becomes evident that quotation marks are required around the terms 'philosopher' and 'philosophy'? Some of Derrida's more hasty readers have seen fit to categorize him as a writer. But what if the term 'writer' (and the related term, 'literature') also demands to be in quotes? As he has remarked: 'I wonder if one can still be altogether a "writer" or a "philosopher". No doubt I am neither one nor the other' (HPH 189).

7 What does it mean to say that so-and-so was born, 'he was born', 'I was born'? Or rather not even 'was', since the verb is perhaps significantly absent here: 'born in 1930'. There is something odd here regarding the sense of tense and time, 'was born', 'is born'. (In French the equivocality is more obvious: *je suis né(e)*, 'I am born' and/or 'I was born'.) What does it mean to be 'born'? In what sense will one ever have known? For Derrida, 'anxiety [can] never be dispelled on this subject' (MMW 339). Every birth is 'an absolute beginning, a different origin of the world': it is a surprise, an event that 'resists even retrospective analysis' (DA 543).

8 'Born in 1930': what is a date? A date is singular, unique. It is 'what does not return, what is not repeated' (TSICL 42); it 'is at once what is inscribed so as to preserve the uniqueness of the moment but what, by the same token, loses it . . . The date is always effaced. Even when it is inscribed, it is effaced' (PTP 378–9). Think of 'September 11' – or of any other date. A date is a strange thing: it is, in Derrida's words, one of those 'codes that we cast like nets over time and space – in order to reduce or master differences, to arrest them, determine them' (AC 419).

9 Finally, the sentence ending with the words 'born in 1930' leaves something unsaid, or something said without being said, it makes a sort of ghostly affirmation, namely that the someone in question

is alive, still living or living on. What does this mean? What does 'living' or 'living on' mean? And what is this ghostliness? What is a ghost? These questions, which are Derrida's, will also be my subject here.

Before we begin, then, we might ask ourselves: what assumptions, beliefs and indeed phantasms or ghosts are already in play, at work, around this question 'Why Derrida?' It might seem obvious we should understand the question as 'Why should there be a book about Derrida?' or 'Why should I want or need to read a book about Derrida?'

This is already to open up two quite different possibilities. The first ('Why should there be a book about Derrida?') is a question that concerns me at least as much as you. The second ('Why should I want or need to read a book about Derrida?') perhaps more concerns you. It would also be difficult to ignore something else going on in the question and in what we might take to be its tone. 'Why Derrida?' is a calling to account and the calling for an account: come on, explain yourself, *why Derrida?* Why should I want or need to know about Derrida? Give an account of why anyone should be interested.

URGENT: SLOW DOWN

I have by now set out a good number of the topics that I will be trying to deal with in the course of this book: the question of responding, the different readings to which a particular question or statement or text can or must give rise, questions of identity (human, sexual, ethnic, religious, national, political, personal) and what Derrida has called the 'disorder of identity', the question of address and tone, and the sense of being called to account, being called to give an account, of being in some sense 'up in front of the authorities', before the law. If there is a guiding dictum for approaching Derrida it would be: slow down. Take care, read (on) slowly. 'Derrida' calls for patience, the sort of patience that the Czech writer Franz Kafka (1883–1924) evokes when he writes, in one of his great aphorisms: 'All human errors are impatience, a premature breaking-off of methodical procedure, an apparent fencing-in of what is apparently at issue' (Kafka 1994, 3).

Like Kafka, Derrida is concerned with a kind of radical patience, a sort of patience concerning every assumption of what is going on in any act of 'fencing-in'. But this does not mean, even for a moment, that

Derrida advocates quietism, inactivity, a studied *laissez faire*. As he has put it: 'It is necessary to defer, to take one's distance, to tarry; but also to rush in precipitately' (DA 533). One has to make decisions: 'absolute urgency', he has more than once remarked, is 'the law of decision' (PF 79). It is precisely for this reason that he is so concerned, everywhere in his writings, with the nature of decision-making and the experience of what he calls the undecidable.

THE UNDECIDABLE

Derrida is careful to distinguish 'undecidability' from 'indeterminacy', characterizing the latter as a kind of 'negativity' or 'nothingness' (ATED 149). Like Kafka, he is fascinated by the concept of the decision, in particular insofar as it necessarily entails an experience of the undecidable, the incalculable and unprogrammable, the un-fence-in-able. As he puts it: there is no decision that is not 'structured by this *experience and experiment of the undecidable*' (ATED 116). The undecidable is never pure: 'no completeness is possible for undecidability' (116). It is not a tool or method to be used or not used. Rather it is a ghostliness that 'render[s] all totalization, fulfilment, plenitude impossible' (116). 'The undecidable remains caught, lodged, at least as a ghost – but an essential ghost – in every decision, in every event of decision' (FL 965). This leads to the formulation of an extraordinary double-question: 'Who will ever be able to assure us that a decision as such has taken place? That it has not . . . followed a cause, a calculation, a rule . . .?' (FL 965). Derrida is concerned to stress and analyse the enigma of decision, the sort of mad blip of any and every decision anyone ever makes or thinks they make. On more than one occasion he has recalled an insight derived from the Danish philosopher Søren Kierkegaard (1813–55): the instant of decision is a madness (see, for instance, CHM 31; FL 967). 'The moment in which the decision is made is heterogeneous to knowing' (TS 61), Derrida says: it is a moment of 'non-knowledge'. All deliberation is over: a decision is the 'imperceptible suspense' (FL 965) of a mad instant.

In order to be worthy of the name, a decision must be structured by the incalculable and un-fence-in-able. In Derrida's terms, we have to reckon with the notion of decision not as 'something active' but rather as a sort of 'passion' (AI 222). His work is an attempt to shift away from thinking of decision in terms of presence, a self-identical calculating 'person-who-decides', the decision as an active act. 'A decision has to be prepared by reflection and knowledge. . . . One has to calculate as far as possible, but the incalculable happens' (TS 61). 'Why Derrida?' Let us try to remain patient while noting that every decision we might make in terms of responding to this question is haunted by an experience of the undecidable and opens onto the incalculable. To adopt a phrase from Derrida, a certain madness must watch over this question (see MMW).

LIVING ON

'Why Derrida?' might have begun to sound a little strange and hollow by now, but I want to try to let it resonate as distinctly, indeed as singularly as possible from the outset. Along with the tone of provocation, the implied impatience, the get-on-with-it-we-are-all-consumers-here, we-don't-have-time, we-want-to-be-told-right-away-why-Derrida, there is perhaps also a more peculiar knell sounding. We may suppose that the question is not intended as a sort of death threat, and yet it is difficult simply to ignore this reading of the question: 'Why does Derrida exist? What purpose does he serve? Couldn't we do perfectly well without him?'

It might appear to be a matter of simply deciding between two interpretations of the name, as if without batting an eyelid: 'Derrida' the bearer of the name, and 'Derrida' the texts, the work; 'Derrida' the 'critical thinker', and 'Derrida' the critical thought, in particular the stuff in print, all the books (authored or co-authored, there are at least seventy of them), and all the essays and interviews. But there is something askew here. If the question 'Why Derrida?' is taken to refer primarily to Derrida's writings, and if we thus politely ignore the sort of death-threat lurking in the title-phrase, we are in a sense carrying out this threat, eliminating Derrida the bearer of the name from our so-called critical thinking. Whichever way we go at it, apparently, the name carries death.

The name carries death. This is a preoccupation that runs throughout Derrida's writings. As he remarks, for example, in the context of a discussion of the German philosopher Friedrich Nietzsche (1844–1900): 'the name, to be distinguished from the bearer, is always and a priori a dead man's name, a name of death' (EO 7). One of the things that most passionately interests Derrida, however, is precisely this question of the distinction between the name and the bearer of the name, which is, at least in some sense, a distinction between death and life. One of the most common misunderstandings of Derrida's work has had to do with the so-called 'death of the author'. The popularity of the phrase 'the death of the author' derives principally from Roland Barthes's 1968 essay of that title (Barthes 1977). Barthes's essay jubilantly proclaims the death of the author in figurative and ideological terms: the time has come to stop reading texts in terms of authorial intention or what we think the author meant by such and such a statement. We must stop referring the source of meaning and authority of a text back to its author (a God-like father-figure), Barthes declares.

Such a proclamation is in many respects contrary to Derrida's concerns. As I hope to make clear in the chapters that follow, he has always been extremely attentive to the importance of what the author means or is trying to say. At least as early as 1976 we can hear Derrida speaking out against the Barthesian phrase, remarking on 'that death or omission of the author of which, as is certainly the case, too much of a case has been made' (S 22). It would perhaps be more apt to say that Derrida is in fact absolutely obsessed with the *life* of the author: we might thus quite reasonably describe his œuvre as a bizarre, ghostly 'Life of the Author' in seventy or more volumes. He is fascinated by the enigmatic nature of autobiography, by the question of survival or 'living on' (see, in particular, LO).

It is not that Derrida has nothing to say about death, the concept of the author or the meeting of the two: on the contrary. As he puts it in an interview in 1995: 'I think about nothing but death, I think about it all the time, ten seconds don't go by without the imminence of the thing being there' (TS 88). But his preoccupation with death is characterized by the fact that he doesn't believe in an afterlife: 'I do not believe that one lives on post-mortem' (TS 88). His abiding focus is on the question of the strangeness of 'death' not as the opposite of life, but rather as something at the very heart of life, as the very condition of thinking and desire, of learning how to live (see SM xvii–xviii). His concern is with trying to think about the strange state of 'disbelief' which we live, or of which we are dying, namely that 'we will never believe either in death or immortality' (M 21). It is a concern with 'the unthought non-self-identity of the concept or the being called "life"' (SM 187), with the sense that 'life' in its essence is *different-from-itself*. In short, it's a ghost's life. (I will come back to all of these perhaps rather obscure-sounding propositions and try to clarify them in due course.)

ANSWERING THE QUESTION: WHY DERRIDA?

'Why Derrida?': I confess that I have not, and will perhaps never have, finished responding to this question. Permit me, however, to offer two preliminary answers. Why should there be a book about Derrida and why might it be helpful?

ANSWER 1

Because we live in the Derridean epoch. Because, more than those of any other contemporary writer or thinker, Derrida's texts have described and transformed the ways in which we think about the nature of language, speech and writing, life and death, culture, ethics, politics, religion, literature and philosophy. More than any other contemporary writer or thinker, Jacques Derrida has defined our time.

The question 'Why Derrida?' is absurd: it makes me smile. There is something at once appalling and hilarious about it. It is like asking 'Why culture?', 'Why education?', 'Why think?' In my apparently bold claim that we live in the Derridean epoch and that Jacques Derrida is the most important thinker of our time, the phrases 'Derridean epoch' and 'our time' should doubtless be in quotation marks. An epoch is 'a point of time fixed or made remarkable by some great event from which dates are reckoned'; 'a time from which a new state of things dates'; 'an age (geological, historical, etc.)' (*Chambers Dictionary*). It comes from the ancient Greek word *epochē* meaning a 'holding up' or 'suspension'. 'Derridean epoch' refers not only to a particular point or period of time (specifically, perhaps, the period dating from the publication in 1967 of three astonishing books – *Of Grammatology*, *Speech and Phenomena* and *Writing and Difference* – up to the present), but also to a conception of the epoch itself, of epochality, time, history and periodicity in Derrida's terms. If Derrida's three books of 1967 are indeed (as the saying goes) epoch-making, it is in part because they entail a new thinking and understanding of what is meant by 'epoch', 'time', 'the present', 'history', 'dates' and other related terms. If Derrida is the great thinker of 'our time', it is because he is concerned with a questioning and rethinking of what the term 'epoch' or the phrase 'our time' could or should mean. He is concerned with the notion of the untimely, with trying to elucidate Hamlet's haunting proposition: 'The time is out of joint' (1.5.196). Above all, Derrida treats terms such as 'epoch' and 'our time' with considerable suspicion. Thus, thinkers such as Kierkegaard and Nietzsche are important to him because they are, as he puts it, 'thinkers of the untimely, who begin by putting into question the interpretation of history as development, in which something that is contemporary to itself – self-contemporary – can succeed something that is past' (TS 6). What Derrida shares with Kierkegaard and Nietzsche, and with Shakespeare's Hamlet, is 'a certain malaise about belonging to a time, to our time – the difficulty of saying "our" time. Our time is perhaps the time in which it is no longer so easy for us to say "our time"' (TS 7). As he asserts at the heart of *Of Grammatology*: 'To make enigmatic what one thinks one understands by the words "proximity", "immediacy" [and] "presence" . . . is my final intention in this book' (OG 70).

This opening section, 'Why Derrida?', might be read as a sort of preface, a supplement to another preface (i.e. to the 'Series editor's preface': see vii–x). A preface, as Derrida has remarked, 'recreates an intention-to-say after the fact'. Having written the rest of the book, I then go back and write a preface as if I haven't yet written the book, or as if the text I have written, which is therefore in the past, can be presented ('under the false appearance of a present', in Derrida's phrase) as 'the future' (O 7; cf. DS 211). The preface 'is an essential and ludicrous operation', Derrida argues, among other things 'because writing as such does not consist in any of these tenses (present, past or future insofar as they are all modified presents)' (O 7). If Derrida's work constitutes a 'strange strategy without finality' (O 7), it is because it changes how we are obliged to think about writing and reading, about the time or times of a text.

Permit me to add one or two remarks here in keeping with the conventional style of a preface, telling you 'under the false appearance of a present' what lies ahead. First of all, I should note that the question of the preface does not go away. The whole of this book will have been 'a preface to reading Derrida', after all. Each chapter in the book will constitute a preface of sorts: with luck it should be possible for the reader to pick up the book and start from more or less any chapter. This, I hope, will accord with the logic, just mentioned, of a 'strategy without finality'.

Second, I should stress that the pages that follow are necessarily idiosyncratic. I seek to be as faithful and scrupulous and attentive to Derrida's texts as possible, but I cannot help going about this in my own particular way. In this respect it may be apposite to remark the understanding (tacit perhaps until now) that 'Why Derrida?' is, in the first place, a question addressed to anyone and everyone *apart from Derrida himself*. Every reading is singular and different. In this context, I should warn you at the outset that my account of Derrida's work will be (in some ways perhaps rather violently) oriented towards literature and literary studies. I will be concerned with describing him primarily as a writer or critical thinker rather than specifically as a philosopher. This is, I hope, not an entirely unfitting way of approaching his work: after all, as he himself said in 1980, 'my most constant interest, coming even before my philosophical interest I should say, if this is possible, has been directed towards literature, towards that writing which is called literary' (TTP 37). In other words, while I hope that this book is faithful to the philosophical import of Derrida's work, it takes its explicit bearings from William Shakespeare (1564–1616) and Emily Brontë (1818–48) rather than from G.W.F. Hegel (1770–1831) and Edmund Husserl (1859–1938). Literature is in any case, for Derrida, indissociably bound up with questions of politics, democracy and responsibility, religion, nationality and nationalism, identity and law. It is by way of the literary, then, that I hope to provide an account of how, more than any other contemporary writer or thinker, Jacques Derrida has defined 'our time' and our 'time out of joint'.

The idiosyncrasy of the present study also has to do with issues of language in, and as, translation. 'Why?' is not 'Pourquoi?' The book that you are reading is in English; it is concerned with transposing or translating Derrida's work into what is called the English language. I shall, on occasion, make reference to the so-called 'original' French wording of Derrida's texts; but my most passionate interest is with the seismic and uncanny effects of his work *in* and *on* the English language. He himself has stressed the notion of translation as 'transformation'. As he states in an interview in 1968: 'for the notion of translation we would have to substitute a notion of *transformation*: a regulated transformation of one language by another, of one text by another' (Pos 20). Translations alter languages. Translation as transformation will also be my subject in what follows. In this way I hope to show that Derrida's work – however slowly, humbly, insidiously – is about changing the English language and about what, 'in changing language, change[s] more than language' (TSICL 55).

'Why Derrida?' Here is one further, final preliminary response to this inexhaustible question.

ANSWER 2

I have no idea. One must have no idea. It is necessary not to know. Contrary to the ludicrous know-all appearance of a preface, writing and reading about Derrida is a matter of reckoning with the incalculable. Perhaps surprisingly, Derrida's thinking in this respect is very close to that of E.M. Forster. As Forster remarks, in his *Aspects of the Novel* (1927), apropos of the experience of writing: 'How can I tell what I think till I see what I say?' (Forster 1976, 99). There can be no response to the question 'Why Derrida?' without a reckoning with what is absolutely unforeseeable, unknowable, incalculable. It is a matter of engaging with the fact that 'there are . . . aleatory or chance elements at work in every kind of message' (EO 108), every kind of text. This question ('Why Derrida?') may indeed be bound up with a conception of the reader as consumer, with that sense of impatience I have been describing, the get-on-with-it-we-are-all-consumers-here and we-want-to-be-told-right-away-why-Derrida; but in order even to begin to understand what Derrida is going on about, it is necessary to recognize in his work a quite different sense of tone and address. This might be illustrated by way of a simple but perhaps unfathomable proposition. Derrida has formulated it explicitly on at least one occasion (see MC 1), but in a sense it guides everything he writes. This proposition would also haunt everything I have said up to now: *I do not know to whom I am speaking.*

2

KEY IDEAS

The preceding pages were supposed to offer some preliminary answers to the question 'Why Derrida?' I tried to suggest a sense of the profound seriousness and importance of the question, as well as its more comical or absurd dimensions. Now I need to explain why the same sort of seriousness and ridiculousness is also to be found in the term 'key ideas'. According to the template for this *Routledge Critical Thinkers* series, first there is a section entitled 'Why [so and so]?'; then there is 'the central section' of the book, which 'discusses the thinker's key ideas, their context, evolution and reception' (p. ix). As I have said, I shall do my utmost to perform this task, in my own manner, and in a manner that seeks to be faithful to the 'critical thinker' in question.

But perhaps the first thing to grasp about Derrida's work is that it shatters the logic of 'key ideas'. If there is a key idea in Derrida it has to do with an interrogation of the 'key idea'. Slow down, I suggested at the outset. Of course there is the desire or need to have summaries, outlines, overviews, paraphrases of this or that thinker or this or that text. But nothing could be less attuned to Derrida as a 'critical thinker' than to pretend his thinking could be arranged as a series of key ideas, to be discussed and summarized one after the other, till we reach the end: at last, phew, the end, no more 'key ideas', that's the lot! Of course we could argue that there is a series of terms that have been closely associated with the name of Derrida: deconstruction, differance, the trace, arche-writing, text, spacing, the supplement, dissemination, undecidability, the hymen, the pharmakon, iterability and so on. (And so on: where would we stop? And why? Enough here perhaps simply to note that one of his 'key ideas' would be the 'and', the 'and so on' or 'et cetera'. 'And in the beginning, there is the *and*': see Etc. 282.) But even these 'terms' are not 'terms' in the sense of something final, self-enclosed, teleological ('term' comes from the French *terme*, a limit, from Latin *terminus*, a boundary). Each of these peculiarly non-terminal terms is part of what Derrida has called an open 'chain of substitutions' (Pos 14). Such 'terms', as he stresses in an interview in 1971, 'are not *atoms*' (Pos 40): they are as much internally divided as they divide. Each is, if you will, a kind of small non-atomic device.

JACQUES IN A BOX

If I were to conform rigidly to the model, template and style of the *Routledge Critical Thinkers* series, I would place boxes (perhaps containing such devices) at more or less regular intervals across these pages. It seems to be an implicit key idea that every book in the series should provide lots of grey boxes containing definitions of 'key terms', or brief accounts of intellectual movements or of other authors. But I shall not be doing this, you may be sorry or glad to hear. Here is, apparently, the only box I propose to offer you. It perhaps encapsulates – and thus explodes – the entire logic of the book (another box) in which it appears to be contained.

What is a box? Is the text in the box separate from the text outside the box? How is it linked? What is the border, the margin or frame? Is it inside or outside the box? And why do we talk of a box, say, rather than a square or oblong, a coffin or crypt? What are we trying to hide? Or what is hereby hiding? 'What is a box?' (TP 229): this is a quotation, a quoted question that might be described as broaching one of the 'key ideas' in Derrida's book *The Truth in Painting* (1978). 'What is the inboxing of a box?' (TP 225), he asks. There is always, he suggests, 'a box *in* the box' and always 'a box *outside* the box' (231). He's talking about Gérard Titus-Carmel's work, *The Pocket Size Tlingit Coffin and the 61 Ensuing Drawings*, but the same logic could be read in and around the present box. As David Wills has put it: 'whatever occurs within the frame can only be contained there by a series of framings, physical, institutional, and discursive, that are held to reside outside it' (Wills 1995, 58). A box is only a box thanks to this duplicity, thanks to 'dimensions' that are and are not part of it. This is the logic of what Derrida elsewhere calls the parergon (in TP 17–147), the border or frame being *both beside* the work (*para + ergon*) *and part of* the work. It is not simply a question of the border lines of a box or frame of a painting, say, but of the borders of texts, institutions, and indeed nations and continents. As Peggy Kamuf has put it: Derrida is 'a thinker without borders, or rather a thinker of the always divisible border, not least the frontiers dividing the world's map into nation-states, or even the natural borders of its continents' (Kamuf 2002, 2). 'The crossing of borders', as Derrida notes in *Aporias* (1993), always assumes the 'institution' of an 'indivisible line' (A 11). 'Customs, police, visa or passport, passenger identification', he declares, 'all of that is established upon this institution'; yet the indivisibility of this line is compromised, impure, internally divided. Borders are strangely problematic (see A 11–12). It is this strangeness that Derrida explores, with such relentless lucidity and patience, throughout his work – not only in relation to the institutions of literature and philosophy, but also in relation to more obviously 'everyday issues' of politics, ethics and responsibility, of personal, cultural and national identity, of democracy and globalization, hospitality and immigration and so on.

DECENTRING

Is the box open or closed, locked or unlocked? What is the key? What is 'key'? *Chambers Dictionary* specifies the following: 'Key, *adj.* of fundamental importance; (of a speech, etc.) expounding the central principle.' A word that has now cropped up twice here is 'central': the phrase 'key ideas' suggests 'central ideas' and these 'central ideas' are to be presented in 'the central section' of the book. Derrida encourages us to be especially wary of the notion of the centre. We cannot get by without a concept of the centre, perhaps, but if one were looking for a single 'central idea' for Derrida's work it might be that of *decentring*.

It is in this very general context that we might situate the significance of 'poststructuralism' and 'deconstruction': in other words, in terms of a decentring, starting with a decentring of the human subject, a decentring of institutions, a decentring of the *logos*. (*Logos* is ancient Greek for 'word', with all its connotations of the authority of 'truth', 'meaning', etc.: 'In the beginning was the Logos [or Word]', as we are informed at the start of the Gospel according to St John.) It is a question of the deconstruction of *logocentrism*, then, in other words of 'the centrism of language in general' (TS 77). In *Specters of Marx* (1993) Derrida sums up the past 100 years as entailing 'the techno-scientific and effective decentring of the earth, of geopolitics, of the *anthropos* in its onto-theological identity or its genetic properties, of the *ego cogito* – and of the very concept of narcissism whose aporias are . . . the explicit theme of deconstruction' (SM 98). For Derrida, this general decentring, especially as regards the *logos*, is something to affirm. As he puts it in an essay entitled 'Ellipsis' (1967): 'Why would one mourn for the centre? Is not the centre, the absence of play and difference, another name for death?' (Ell 297) Derrida's constant concern has been with what he calls, at the end of 'Structure, Sign, and Play in the Discourse of the Human Sciences' (1966), an '*affirmation [that] determines the noncentre otherwise than as loss of the centre*' (SSP 292).

What one repeatedly finds in Derrida's work is the uncanny effect by which one is invited to sense the unfolding of all of his thinking starting out from anywhere, from any idea, any word, any thought that happens to be at issue. 'Deconstruction' is perhaps the best-known word for this. It is suitably ironic, in this respect, that I have chosen to offer you a detailed account of deconstruction in the next chapter, but find it already haunting and disturbing the present account of 'key ideas'. Deconstruction is what happens. In some sense its effects are always already going on. As I will try to show in more detail as I go on, deconstruction engages a thinking of the force of the non-centre. This is not to suggest that the concept of the centre is not important. On the contrary, Derrida is sharply aware of this importance: his concern is with describing and transforming it. Centre goes together with structure: as he has remarked, 'the notion of a structure lacking any centre represents the unthinkable itself' (SSP 279). Deconstruction wouldn't make much sense without the structures that are subject to destructuring.

HOW NOT TO THINK ABOUT 'KEY IDEAS'

If I have already begun to talk about 'deconstruction' (the focus of Chapter 3), I have done something similar with the notion of the supplement (the focus of Chapter 5). As we will see in greater detail in due course, all of Derrida's work can be thought about in terms of the notion of the supplement, of what is strangely *extra*, added on (like a preface:

see Chapter 1). My aim in this book is to highlight the supplementary logic whereby *any* word or phrase can be transformed into a 'key idea' in relation to Derrida (or potentially of course any other 'critical thinker'). At the same time, any such 'key' will always turn a lock. Of the 'key', Derrida has appositely remarked: 'Like all keys, it locks and unlocks, opens and closes' (LO 146). Let me briefly summarize some of the more obvious characteristics and connotations of this phrase 'key ideas'.

1   The phrase 'key ideas' has the attraction of a kind of comfortable vagueness and impressionism, as if it is really simply a case of giving you the 'rough idea'.
2   The phrase also sounds comfortingly cerebral, as if Derrida's ideas, key or not, are after all 'just' ideas – exciting, difficult, even head-banging perhaps, but with no real connection to the so-called outside world.
3   The phrase 'key idea' implies a kind of discreteness: here is one idea, and then over there is another one, each one of them self-contained, as if in a little box of its own.
4   The phrase 'key idea' has strong connotations of centre and presence, of something present to oneself, to one's mind, in one's head. ('Wait! I have an idea!' or 'Look, to get to the heart or centre of the matter, here is the key idea!')
5   The phrase is easily construed in terms of ownership. ('I have an idea and it belongs to me: it's my idea!')

Derrida's work consistently queries and disturbs all of these characteristics. There is nothing vague or impressionistic about his work. His concern is to respond to a text or situation with the utmost rigour and clarity. If we are to talk in terms of his 'ideas', key or otherwise, these ideas are in the world, changing the world. As he has consistently argued, 'deconstruction interferes with solid structures, "material" institutions, and not only with discourses or signifying representations' (TP 19). The law of the supplement means that no 'key idea' is definitively separable from another in Derrida's work and nor is it therefore essentially 'key'. So 'the supplement' is itself only one way of talking about this 'key idea of no key idea': it depends on the context, in particular on what text, situation, etc., is being analysed.

WHOSE IDEA WAS THIS?

As Derrida has put it: 'everything depends upon contexts which are always open, non-saturable' (M 115). The supplement, the pharmakon, the hymen or whatever-we-happen-to-find-ourselves-responding-to-next-in-Derrida's-work, are not 'ideas' that are simply present: they are not of the order of presence and they are not simply ours for the having. Derrida elaborates the notion of the supplement (at once that which is added on as a further enrichment and that which is supposed to make up for something that was missing) through a reading of the work of the French novelist, philosopher and educationist Jean-Jacques Rousseau (1712–78) (in OG). He elaborates the notion of the pharmakon (a Greek 'term' that signifies, among other things, both 'remedy' and 'poison') through a reading of the ancient Greek philosopher Plato (c. 428–347 BC) (in PP). He elaborates the notion of the hymen (as both 'virginal membrane' and 'marriage', and thus as figuring that which is undecidably 'between desire and fulfilment') through a reading of the French poet Stéphane Mallarmé (1842–98) (in DS: here, DS 212–13).

The concept of the supplement is not Derrida's, but neither is it simply Rousseau's; the 'pharmakon' is not Derrida's, but neither is it simply Plato's; 'hymen' is not Derrida's, but neither is it simply Mallarmé's. Of course Derrida does things with these concepts, things that are not necessarily attributable to the authorial intentions of Rousseau, Plato or Mallarmé. (Though this does not mean that Derrida thinks 'authorial intention' is something that can or should be brushed to one side: on the contrary, as I hope will become clearer as we go on.) This is precisely the point about contexts always being open and non-saturable. As Derrida stresses in *Of Grammatology* (1967): an author can always be understood to be saying 'more, less, or something other than what he [or she] *would mean*' (OG 158).

No author can ever fully control the ways in which their text might be read. This point may allow me to offer one final word of caution in relation to the desire for a snappy excursion tour around 'Derrida's key ideas'. The logic of authorial blindness that he analyses in *Of Grammatology* also means that it is necessary to reckon with the 'key idea' that Derrida's own 'key ideas' may not yet be known, either to himself or to any other present-day reader. If he has managed to show that the supplement is one of Rousseau's 'key ideas' (with all the reservations and hesitations around that phrase), we might quite reasonably suppose that at least some of Derrida's 'key ideas' may not become evident for another hundred or couple of hundred years.

3

DECONSTRUCTION
THE EARTHQUAKE

Let us recall Answer 1 to the question 'Why Derrida?' More effectively than those of any other contemporary writer, I suggested, his texts describe and transform the ways in which we think about the world, about life, death, culture, philosophy, literature, politics and so on. I would like to say a little more now about the perhaps rather innocuous-sounding phrase 'describe and transform'. There is something a bit cryptic about it. What, you may wonder, is the relationship between describing and transforming? Surely these two things are opposites? To describe something is to treat it (whatever it may be, life, a literary text, a political situation) as pre-existing the description: in describing, you offer a statement about how things already are. To transform, we might suppose, is quite a different business: indeed, it may seem odd to say that texts can transform anything at all. How, we may ask ourselves, can a text transform? A text is surely just lifeless, inert, printed matter?

DESCRIPTION AND TRANSFORMATION

'Text' has a special sense in Derrida's work – and we will come to this later – but for now I would like to say something about this apparently odd couple, 'to describe' and 'to transform'. They offer, I think, a way into the heart of what Derrida is about. He has a longstanding interest in what is known as 'speech act theory'. This interest could be said to pervade everything he has said or written, but it became an explicit focus of his work with the essay 'Signature Event Context' (SEC), originally presented as a lecture in Montreal in August 1971. Speech act theory is most closely associated with the work of the Oxford philosopher J.L. Austin (1911–60), and above all with his remarkable book, *How To Do Things With Words* (1975 [1962]). Austin works with the extremely productive notion that all sorts of utterance or speech act, in other words everything we may say, can be considered in terms of two categories, namely the constative and the performative.

A constative utterance is a statement of how things are, an apparent statement of fact. Thus we can consider a straightforward descriptive statement as constative. 'I am trying to write a book about the work of Jacques Derrida' or 'You are reading these words' would be examples of constative statement. A performative statement or utterance, on the other hand, is perhaps at first glance a more peculiar kettle of fish. A performative utterance is when you not only say something but *do something by saying it*. As examples of performative utterances we might think of promises, threats, prayers, confessions, benedictions, maledictions, challenges, bets, declarations of love or war, fatwa or jihad, acts of naming (for example, with the baptism of a child or the launching of a ship) or acts of founding (for example the Declaration of Independence that legally and historically gives birth to the United States of America). Performative utterances, in short, don't just describe, they transform things, or at least they seek to do so. As Austin puts it, in his characteristically twisting but precise prose: in the case of performative utterances, 'it seems clear that to utter the sentence (in, of course, the appropriate circumstances) is not to *describe* my doing of what I should be said in so uttering to be doing or to state that I am doing it: it is to do it' (Austin 6). If, in response to a certain kind of question, at a particular moment of a marriage service, I say 'I do', I am committing myself to something that is in principle lifelong and that changes the way things are for good, or at any rate (as the saying goes) for better or for worse. If one state declares war on another state, this is a performative: this performative utterance transforms, it alters the way things are, it calls for action and response, on the part of both states.

When I say that Derrida's texts have described and transformed the ways in which we think, partly what I have in mind is this distinction between the constative and the performative. On the one hand, Derrida proceeds with great patience – and (to the evident irritation of many) with great pleasure – to describe what is going on in a particular text or situation. He is an extraordinarily precise and faithful reader. In a quite disarming way, Derrida's readings – for instance, of Plato's *Phaedrus* and related works (in PP), Shakespeare's *Romeo and Juliet* (*c.* 1595) (in AC), Kafka's 'Before the Law' (1914) (in B), Freud's *Beyond the Pleasure Principle* (1920) (in SF) or the American Declaration of Independence (1776) (in DI) – can often appear to be just describing what is happening in that text. If we wanted or rather if we were able to stop things there, this alone would constitute an excellent reason why we should read Derrida: he is a marvellously sharp and attentive reader, a brilliant explicator of texts. It is a journalistic or class-room cliché to say that Derrida is 'difficult'. But we could also see this the other way round. Always remarkably careful, painstaking and scrupulous in his readings, he offers superb expositions and elucidations of philosophical and other texts that are themselves 'difficult'. Would anyone want to pretend that reading Plato or Shakespeare or Freud is 'easy'? Derrida helps us read and make sense of the great, and less great, texts of western history. On the other hand, he transforms the ways in which we are obliged to think about the texts he reads. Juliet's speech on the balcony ('O Romeo, Romeo, wherefore art thou Romeo? . . . What's in a name?' [2.1.75–91]) isn't the same again after Derrida. The same goes for Plato's *Phaedrus* (in PP), or the poetry of Francis Ponge (1899–1988) (in S) or James Joyce's *Ulysses* (1922) (in UG).

DEFINING DECONSTRUCTION

Derrida, then, describes and transforms. It is this strange, even contradictory combination of description and transformation that will perhaps help me to clarify the word with which Derrida's work is perhaps most frequently identified: deconstruction. It is probably worth noting that Derrida himself has no great fondness for the word. As he puts it in his thesis-defence, in 1980: '["deconstruction"] is a word I have never liked and one whose fortune has disagreeably surprised me' (TTP 44). He is alluding here to the ways in which, especially in the late 1970s and 1980s (and especially in the US), deconstruction came to be understood by many as a critical method or tool. People spoke of the 'Yale School' of deconstruction (for critical discussions of this, see for example Arac, Godzich and Martin 1983; Davis and Schleifer 1985); 'deconstruction' was taken to be an *ism*. Here we might usefully take note of a comment made by the contemporary critic and theorist Martin McQuillan: 'deconstruction is not a school or an "ism". There is no such thing as "deconstructionism": this is a word used by idiots' (McQuillan 2000, 41). It would be perfectly possible to write a book about Derrida's work without making use of the word 'deconstruction'. But if I were to do so, you might feel hard done by. So here are a couple of dictionary-style definitions. First, from the 1989 edition of the *Oxford English Dictionary*:

deconstruction [f. DE + CONSTRUCTION]

a. The action of undoing the construction of a thing.

b. *Philos.* And *Lit. Theory.* A strategy of critical analysis associated with the French philosopher Jacques Derrida (b. 1930), directed towards exposing unquestioned metaphysical assumptions and internal contradictions in philosophical and literary language.

And here is a more recent definition which, as you might be able to guess, does not come from a dictionary:

deconstruction n. not what you think: the experience of the impossible: what remains to be thought: a logic of destabilization always already on the move in 'things themselves': what makes every identity at once itself and different from itself: a logic of spectrality: a theoretical and practical parasitism or virology: what is happening today in what is called society, politics, diplomacy, economics, historical reality, and so on: the opening of the future itself.

(Royle 2000, 11)

I will leave these definitions for you to ponder, merely noting for the moment that each of them is in fact *plural*. There is, as Derrida has remarked, no 'univocal definition' or 'adequate description' for this strange event called deconstruction, and the reason for 'this absence of univocal definitions is not "obscurantist"' (ATED 141), but rather it is linked to what he calls a new enlightenment (about which I shall say more anon). Of these dictionary-style definitions, then, let me in passing simply note that the first (from the *OED*) is specifically focused on 'philosophical and literary language', whereas the second proposes that deconstruction is everywhere, not simply in the realms of philosophy or literature, and indeed not merely in 'language'.

Deconstruction is, as Derrida has often said, 'what happens' ('*ce qui arrive*': see, for example, SST 85; TS 64). On numerous occasions, perhaps starting with the amazing early essay 'Force and Signification' (1963), Derrida has spoken of what impels his writing as a trembling, a 'shaking' or 'soliciting' (FS 6). He has written again and again, but always differently, about 'producing a force of dislocation that spreads itself throughout the entire system' (FS 20), about deconstruction as 'de-sedimentation' (OG 10), about a force of irruption that '[disorganizes] the entire inherited order' (Pos 42). Deconstruction is an earthquake.

SEISMIC COMMUNICATIONS

The earthquake can show up in the smallest crack, the slightest tremor. Deconstruction involves a seismological attentiveness to the tiniest details. It happens in relation to a specific context, even if the crack or fissure detected opens up into a far more general effect. In historical and genealogical terms, Derrida's elaboration of 'deconstruction' is inextricably bound up with the importance and effects of the writings of Nietzsche (1844–1900), Freud (1856–1939) and Heidegger (1889–1976). (I discuss this further in Chapter 7.) But to phrase matters in this way is already in danger of misleading. Deconstruction begins, among other things, with a profound wariness concerning proper names. In *Of Grammatology* (1967), for example, Derrida remarks that 'it would be frivolous to think that "Descartes", "Leibniz", "Rousseau", "Hegel", etc. are names of authors': rather, he says, each is in the first place 'the name of a problem' (OG 99). This is also one reason why the business of writing the present book is so tricky: I have to make claims about 'Derrida's work' or 'Derrida in general', knowing that this is in a sense a very undeconstructive gesture, but hoping that you will appreciate its strategic usefulness as a means of encouraging you to go on to look at 'Derrida's work' in specific texts and contexts. In an interview in 1993 he remarks:

> [D]econstruction moves, or makes its gestures, lines and divisions move, not only within the corpus [of a writer] in general, but at times within a single sentence, or a microscopic element of a corpus. Deconstruction mistrusts proper names: it will not say 'Heidegger in general' says thus or so; it will deal, in the micrology of the Heideggerian text, with different moments, different applications, concurrent logics, while trusting no generality and no configuration that is solid and given. It is a sort of great earthquake, a general tremor,

which nothing can calm. I cannot treat a corpus, or a book, as a whole, and even the simple statement is subject to fission.

(TS 9)

Even the most apparently simple statement is subject to fission or fissure. This is deconstruction as destabilization always already on the move within. 'There is no atom' (Dia 137), as Derrida remarks in what is one of his most succinct and most quietly, subterraneously explosive formulations. Everything is divisible. Unity, coherence, univocality are effects produced out of division and divisibility. This is what gives rise to the elaboration of terms such as differance, iterability, the trace, the supplement: we will come to consider each of these in due course.

So Derrida's work is about earthquake phenomena or 'seismisms'. (One of his biggest mouthfuls of an essay-title is 'Some Statements and Truisms about Neo-Logisms, Newisms, Postisms, Parasitisms, and other Small Seismisms' [SST]). It is about shaking up, dislocating and transforming the verbal, conceptual, psychological, textual, aesthetic, historical, ethical, social, political and religious landscape. Its concern is to disturb, to de-sediment, to deconstruct. But these seismic transformations are in crucial ways always already in the texts he reads. In a sense he does little more than describe what happens when reading, say, a passage of Shakespeare or a Plato dialogue or a short story by Kafka. Hence the strange notion of describing and transforming. As Derrida has said: 'everything is in Shakespeare . . . in Plato . . . or in Kafka' (TSICL 67). In a sense, it is just a matter of what happens when you describe it. This no doubt makes the thing sound too formalistic, as if deconstruction (or what Derrida does) were simply a technique or a method. It is crucial to understand that this is not the case. The relation between 'description' and 'transformation' is uncanny, I would like to suggest. Deconstruction is uncanny. (For a more extended account of deconstruction and the uncanny, see Royle 2003.)

The strangeness has to do as much as anything else with the 'and' of 'description and transformation'. As Derrida has commented in an essay on the word 'and': 'Wondering what the "*and*" *is*, what *and* . . . means and does not mean, does and does not do . . . is perhaps . . . the most constant task of any deconstruction' (Etc. 285). To attend to the deconstructive effects of the 'and' (which would be another way of starting to talk about the logic of the supplement) is to reckon with the consequences of the fact that the distinction between description *and* transformation, or between constative *and* performative, is never stable. We encounter what Derrida has called, in the context of an analysis of the US Declaration of Independence, an 'undecidability between . . . a performative structure and a constative structure' (DI 9). Concerning the Declaration of Independence, drafted by Jefferson and signed by the 'representatives of the United States in General Congress assembled . . . in the name and by the authority of the good people', Derrida's interest lies in the fact that 'one cannot decide . . . whether independence is stated or produced by this utterance' (DI 9). This is the perspective from which Derrida's own texts seek to be read. He is driven by the desire

> to invent something new in the form of acts of writing which no longer consist in a theoretical knowledge, in new constative statements, to give oneself to a poetico-literary performativity at least analogous to that of promises, orders, or acts of constitution or legislation which do not only change language, or which, in changing language, change more than language.
>
> (TSICL 55)

It is a desire to describe *and* transform, undecidably; to put into effect new kinds of discourses, acts and institutions. Such description and transformation has to do with language *and* with 'more than language'. This indeed is one of the ways in which Derrida has tentatively defined 'deconstruction': as '*plus d'une langue* – both more than a language and no more of *a* language' (M 15).

There are always differences, tensions, paradoxes between what a text says (or what an author wants to say, or thinks s/he is saying) and what a text does. What especially intrigues Derrida about Austin's account of how to do things with words is his sense that Austin's analysis 'is often more fruitful in the acknowledgement of its impasses than in its positions' (SEC 14). In particular what he draws out of his reading of Austin is an acknowledgement of the fact that 'there is no "pure" performative' (SEC 17). A performative can always fail. This is perhaps especially easy to see in the case of the promise: if I promise (and I hereby do solemnly promise) to provide you, in due course, with an account of Derrida's work in relation to 'literature', 'the gift', 'the signature', 'the law', 'secrets' and 'drugs', it is always possible that this promise will not be kept. It is always possible that I am not being serious or that I am lying when I make my promise. These possibilities of a promise not being fulfilled (I might die before I finish writing this book, you might die before you finish reading it, I might just have been joking or pretending when I made my promise, etc.) – these possibilities are not accidental or 'beside the point', in Derrida's view: rather, they are necessary possibilities.

FUNNY STUFF

In order for a promise to be a promise it must be non-fulfillable. It is a structurally *necessary possibility* that the promise might turn out not to be realized. Hence the argument that there is no 'pure' performative. This 'failure' at the heart of the performative utterance is not so much an accident waiting to happen as an essential condition of any performative at all. The performative is haunted by what is indeed unthinkable ('death' is perhaps the quickest, but also perhaps most cryptic shorthand for it). There is thus what Derrida elsewhere calls an 'irremediable disturbance or perversion' that is 'within the very structure of the *act* of promising'. At the same time, he proposes that this sense of an internal upset also accounts for 'the *unbelievable*, and comical, aspect of every promise' (M 94).

So Derrida seeks to be 'exceedingly scrupulous and exceedingly serious' (LI 65), but he is also a very funny writer: this is one of the things that some people evidently find infuriating about him. It is difficult not to feel that he is doing something strange with words: language can come to seem like very funny stuff. We may rightly feel that, to borrow a haunting formulation from one of his essays on psychoanalysis, 'a certain foreign body is here working over our household words' (F xxv). It is the 'non-serious' (Austin 22, SEC 16), and in particular the *necessary possibility* of the 'non-serious', that Derrida finds haunting Austin's account of how to do things with words. Provokingly, this 'non-seriousness' is, for Austin, closely identified with *literature*. It may very well take the form of fiction, acting, or (perhaps most oddly) a poem. Thus Austin writes of what is happening when I say 'I promise to . . .':

Surely the words must be spoken 'seriously' and so as to be taken 'seriously'? This is, though vague, true enough in general – it is an important commonplace in discussing the purport of any utterance whatsoever. I must not be joking, for example, nor writing a poem.

(Austin 9)

In picking up on what Austin seems to be intent on excluding from his account (here the poetic or 'not serious'), Derrida does things with Austin's words that Austin's words are in some important sense already doing themselves, even if Austin would perhaps not wholeheartedly subscribe to them.

Derrida is not interested in having a joke at Austin's expense: he recognizes that Austin is not only a fascinating and profoundly original philosophical thinker but also, like Derrida, in various respects a very witty writer as well. Derrida is not primarily interested, indeed, in the successes or triumphs of doing things with words as such. His interest in speech act theory has rather to do with experiences of failure, weakness, the improper or supposedly excluded or 'inappropriate'. He is fascinated by the notion that what is most powerful is 'often the most disarming feebleness' (TSICl 59; cf. TS 64). If it is a necessary possibility that a performative can fail, there is no performative that is not haunted by this failure, this disturbance or perversion. It is for this reason that Derrida has sought to describe and transform the 'traditional' notion of the performative by invoking the notion of the *perverformative* (see, for example, E 136). Derrida would doubtless concur with Austin that speech act theory figures a sort of 'revolution in philosophy' (Austin 3) but for him it would be a revolution of a perverformative sort.

Every performative is spooky and perverse, haunted by the unthinkable or 'death'. Derrida's concern is to elaborate a new theory and practice of the performative, a kind of thinking 'dissociated from the notion of presence that people always attach to the performative' (LO 146). This is why – as we shall see in greater detail as we go on – the earthquake effects of deconstruction are at once ghostly *and* real.

4

BE FREE

Imagine some graffiti on a wall somewhere that reads simply: 'BE FREE'. These two words provide a striking example of what Derrida calls a double bind (TNOF 203). As an order, 'be free' tells you to be what you cannot be except in obeying this order: to obey the order to 'be free' is not to be free. You are free to do anything as long as you accept that you are not free to disobey what I am hereby ordering you. Come on, be free. But is it an order, in fact? Who is the 'I' here? And who is the reader or addressee of this piece of graffiti transplanted from an imaginary wall on to the page in front of you? In grammatical terms we could describe the words 'be free' as an imperative. As the author of *How To Do Things With Words* points out, however, 'an "imperative" may be an order, a permission, a demand, a request, an entreaty, a suggestion, a recommendation, a warning . . . or may express a condition or concession or a definition' (Austin 76–7).

'BE FREE': at what point will we have finished reading this, so that we can be free? Or in what sense could we ever be free enough to read it at all? 'Be free': I would like to invite you to think about this as one of Derrida's so-called key ideas. As such, it engages with the question of his commitment to a sort of 'responsible anarchy', a commitment entailing an 'interminable' questioning of the concept of responsibility itself and of the law or laws that make it possible to think the meaning of 'anarchy' (a word deriving from the ancient Greek, *anarchia*, 'leaderlessness', 'lawlessness'): see DO 120–1. Derrida's work is driven by a desire for momentous revolutionary change, even for 'unimaginable revolution' (SM 82). 'The world is going very badly' (SM 77–8), as he stresses throughout that 'essay in the night' called *Specters of Marx* (1993).

The world could be so entirely different. Everything can be rethought: politics, ethics, religion, literature, philosophy, culture, society, identity and subjectivity, nationalism and internationalism. There must be freedom for everyone: 'be free', everyone. This is what he is getting at with the notions of what he calls the 'democracy to come' (TSICL 38, OH 78), a 'new enlightenment' (ATED 141, DA 37) and the 'new international' (SM 85–6).

In an apparently paradoxical fashion, Derrida is at the same time also an avowedly conservative thinker, in the sense that he wants to 'keep things' and to preserve memory. He loves history; he has a deep respect for tradition, for the so-called western literary and philosophical canons, and so on. At issue is a double gesture: on the one hand 'emancipation, revolt, irony', on the other 'scrupulous fidelity' (TS 43). As he puts it: 'I feel best when my sense of emancipation preserves the memory of what it emancipates from. I hope this mingling of respect and disrespect for the academic heritage and tradition in general is legible in everything I do' (TS 43). This double gesture (respect and disrespect, fidelity and violation, preservation and emancipation, description and transformation) pervades Derrida's work.

REINVENTING PLAY

'Be free': this phrase might also evoke the notion of so-called 'free play'. Derrida has often been associated with 'virtuoso dazzling textual performances' demonstrating the 'subversive effects' of 'linguistic free play'. I am not quoting anyone in particular here, but rather recalling a few of the dreary clichés especially prevalent in Anglophone academic critical writing on Derrida in the 1980s. The term 'linguistic free play' is not his. His whole point is that there is no pure freedom or play, and that the distinctions between what is linguistic and what is non-linguistic are more complex and strange than have traditionally been understood. As I hope to make clear, while Derrida is of course deeply interested in the nature and possibilities of language, this entails at the same time a constant preoccupation with what he variously evokes as the 'other of language' (FS 27), a notion of the other as that which is 'beyond language and which summons language' (DO 123).

All of this is not to suggest that Derrida's writings are without inventiveness: on the contrary, they are so inventive that they seek to 'reinvent invention' (PIO 60). They are indeed very often extraordinary in 'form', 'style' and 'content' (to use three terms whose intelligibility and status his texts systematically question and disturb). 'Play', for Derrida, is never 'simply playing' (EO 69), anymore than it is for a child. But this also means that play can be 'very risky' in ways that a child would not understand. Derrida is concerned with trying 'to think of play in a radical way', in a way that goes 'beyond the activity of a subject manipulating objects according to or against the rules, etc.' (EO 69). The inventiveness of his work calls for a thinking of language as not 'merely' human, and a thinking of invention no longer in terms of 'accrediting a priori the opposition between animals and men that serves as the basis for the current values of invention' (PIO 64; see also ATED 134).

Perhaps more readily than its English so-called equivalent, the French word *jeu* suggests both 'play' and 'give'. To begin to get a sense of 'play' in Derrida, then, we should be thinking about it, as he says,

> not simply in the sense of the ludic, but also in the sense of that which, by the spacing between the pieces of an apparatus, allows for movement and articulation – which is to say, for history, for better or for worse. This play is sometimes what allows the machine to function normally, but sometimes the same word designates an articulation that is too loose, without rigor, the cause of an anomaly or a pathological malfunctioning.
>
> (TSICL 64)

'Play', as he puts it at the end of his celebrated essay 'Structure, Sign, and Play in the Discourse of the Human Sciences' (1966), 'is the disruption of presence'. It is a play 'without security' (SSP 292). So if we want to think of Derrida as 'playing with language', we would need to understand this in a distinct and decidedly strange fashion. 'Playing with language' is never simply 'playing with language' (LO 80). In *Of Grammatology*, Derrida asserts: '[logocentrism] has always placed in parentheses, *suspended*, and suppressed for essential reasons, all free reflection on the origin and status of writing' (OG 43). In doing so, he opens up the question of what such 'free reflection' might look like. Will we ever be up to reading these words, 'be free'?

Derrida's deepest concern is, as he has put it, to transform, to 'make something happen to [the French] language' (MO 51). Correspondingly, the translation, reading and so-called reception of his work in English is indissociably bound up with making something happen to the English language. Derrida's work embodies and communicates a revolutionary desire to read and write texts that 'in changing language, change more than language' (TSICL 55); but at the same time also a desire to preserve memory and tradition. So, if you are approaching Derrida's work with the expectation of linguistic 'free play', for example, bear in mind also the converse of this. Derrida is the one who baldly states: 'I detest grammatical mistakes' (TS 43). It is Derrida who argues that what might in some ways seem to be his most 'linguistically playful' work, *Glas*, contains 'not one single *pun*' (Pro 17). It is he who indeed dreams of being the guardian, the 'last heir, the last defender and illustrator of the French language' (MO 47).

A NEW ENLIGHTENMENT

In the context of Derrida's work, 'be free' (or, in a somewhat scandalous formulation in French: *libère*, 'liberate yourself, you and the others': see OH 60) would be bound up with a thinking of democracy. 'Be free', as I have been trying to suggest, only makes sense in terms of a relation to law, however paradoxical and deconstructible that may be. Derrida's work is impelled by a desire 'for what, in politics, is called republican democracy as a universalizable model, binding philosophy to the public "cause"' (FK 8). He is committed to what he has called a new enlightenment, one that does not forget the European Enlightenment or *Aufklärung* associated with the philosophy of Immanuel Kant (1724–1804), but that nevertheless marks itself out differently, one that affirms a different step or gait, a different movement, process or 'bearing' (*démarche* is Derrida's word here: see AT 60). There is something apocalyptic about Derrida's writings, about the 'tone' of his work as well as the arguments. More particularly, Derrida's apocalypticism aims at showing up a derailment that has always already taken place in the structure of so-called apocalyptic discourse. (For a detailed example of this, you might like to consider his painstaking reading of Francis Fukuyama's work *The End of History* (1992) in *Specters of Marx* (SM).)

It is not a question of obscurantism, but (however 'enigmatic' the desire for this) of more light. As Derrida writes in the great essay 'Of an Apocalyptic Tone' (originally given as a lecture in 1980):

In the light of today we cannot not have become the heirs of these *Lumières* [Kant and others]. We cannot and we must not – this is a law and a destiny – forgo the *Aufklärung*, in other words, what imposes itself as the enigmatic desire for vigilance, for the lucid vigil, for elucidation, for critique and truth, but for a truth that at the same time keeps within itself some apocalyptic desire, this time as desire for clarity and revelation, in order to demystify or, if you prefer, to deconstruct apocalyptic discourse itself and with it everything that speculates on vision, the imminence of the end, theophany, parousia [ancient Greek for 'presence' or 'arrival', especially the arrival or second coming of Christ], the last judgment.

(AT 51)

It is in this way that Derrida seeks to make a distinction between deconstruction and 'a simple progressive demystification in the style of the Enlightenment' (AT 60). He wishes to question and disturb notions of teleology (all kinds of thinking oriented by a *telos*, i.e. the ancient Greek word for 'end', 'goal' or 'purpose'), of 'progress' with a fixed and definitive goal or purpose. 'Teleology', as he has remarked elsewhere, 'is, at bottom, the negation of the future, a way of knowing beforehand the form that will have to be taken by what is still to come' (TS 20).

FAITH IN DECONSTRUCTION

Deconstruction, on the contrary, is a 'strange strategy without finality' (O 7). It encourages a critical questioning of any and all kinds of religious or political discourse that make dogmatic assumptions about the nature of presence and what might be meant by 'the end'. Derrida's commitment to a new enlightenment thus entails an affirmation of what he has called 'the enlightened virtue of public space, emancipating it from all external power (non-lay, non-secular), for example from religious dogmatism, orthodoxy or authority (that is, from a certain rule of *doxa* or of belief, which, however, does not mean from all faith)' (FK 8).

Derrida is concerned with a radical thinking of faith, stressing that 'faith has not always been and will not always be identifiable with

religion [or] with theology' (FK 8). In particular he is interested in the
nature and effects of what he calls 'faith in language' (MO 85). This
strange fidelity is presupposed even in cases of 'perjury, lying or infidelity'. As he puts it: 'I cannot lie without believing and making believe
in language' (MO 85). (For more on the importance of notions of lying,
perjury and so on, see, for example, Dem and WA.) Language has
already engaged faith before anyone tells the truth or tells a lie. There
is a faith, a strange structure of promise, which haunts everything we
say. As always in Derrida, it is a question of trying to reckon with the
fact that 'language is not the governable instrument of a speaking being
(or subject)' (M 96). The promise is not ours to make but rather perhaps
what makes 'us'. He is preoccupied with the idea that 'promising is
inevitable as soon as we open our mouths' (M 98), in other words that
'there is no speaking that does not promise', no speaking that does not
carry with it 'a commitment toward the future' (M 97). This notion of
the promise is linked, for Derrida, to a new thinking of freedom,
preceding and exceeding any traditional politics or religion. It entails
what he has called 'a rebellious force of affirmation', a promise of liberation from the very 'lexicon of liberation' insofar as this latter 'belongs
to the so-called political register dominated by values of "person", "self"
[and] even of the "body" as referential identity' (V 163).

'Be free': as an aphoristic summary of Derrida's work, this involves
thinking about the apocalyptic and messianic in quite singular respects.
His work is apocalyptic (we should perhaps here recall the etymology of
'apocalypse', from the ancient Greek for 'unveiling' or 'revelation'), but
it is an apocalypticism that questions ends, goals and purposes, an apocalypticism that is wary of any final revelation. Indeed it is an apocalypticism concerned with 'what will have remained alien, for all time, to the
veiled figure, to the very figure of the veil' (MO 73). (This involves, as
we will see later, a different thinking of the concept of the secret and
secrecy.) Correspondingly, Derrida's work is messianic, but this is 'a
messianism without religion, even a messianic without messianism' (SM
59). This messianic has to do with the promise, the 'rebellious force of
affirmation' that sets everything off. It is concerned with a 'formal structure of promise' that at once 'exceeds' and 'precedes' both Marxism and
the religions that Marxism criticizes (SM 59). It is worth noting here that
this notion of promise is not deconstructive: rather, it is what makes
deconstruction possible. As Derrida remarks: 'what remains irreducible
to any deconstruction, what remains as undeconstructible as the possi-

bility itself of deconstruction is, perhaps, a certain experience of the emancipatory promise' (SM 59). The 'emancipatory' here might help-fully be understood with reference to the etymological force of the word as signifying dispossession. (The English word 'emancipation' comes from the Latin ēmancipāre, from ē away from, and mancipāre to transfer property.) There is no subject or messiah, no promiser or promisee who precedes such a promise. This promise bespeaks, as it were, an emanci-pation prior to any property or theft.

COME

Deconstruction can perhaps be distinguished from other kinds of 'enlightenment thinking' in terms of a certain tone, or in terms of an attentiveness to a certain tone. One of the most wonderful passages in all of Derrida's work comes at the end of his essay on apocalyptic tone (AT 62–7), in a meditation on the word 'come'. He explores the sense of this 'come' as it appears in the Book of Revelation, the Revelation or Apocalypse of St John. 'Come' keeps coming, coming in and coming back in the course of the last book of the Bible: why? and how should we hear or understand it? 'He which testifieth these things saith, Surely I come quickly. Amen. Even so, come, Lord Jesus' (Rev. 22: 20; cf. AT 64). Derrida's discussion of this word 'come' – 'if it is a word' (AT 62) – bears witness to one of his most abiding and fundamental concerns, that is to say a ghostliness in the voice.

There are many critics and other readers who see Derrida as someone who is forever going on about writing; there remains a widespread con-ception, or rather misconception, that he has it in for what is supposedly the opposite of *writing*, namely speech. Isn't that what all the fuss about 'phonocentrism' (literally, voice-centredness, a centrism of the voice or speech) boils down to, an attack on the privileging of voice and speech, a privileging that occurs – and has occurred throughout 'the whole history of metaphysics' (SP 16) – at the expense of writing? In *Speech and Phenomena* and *Of Grammatology*, for example, Derrida has indeed produced deconstructive readings of phonocentric aspects of Jean-Jacques Rousseau (1712–78), Ferdinand de Saussure (1857–1913), Edmund Husserl (1859–1938) and Claude Lévi-Strauss (1908–), focus-ing on the innumerable ways in which 'phonocentrism merges with the historical determination of the meaning of being in general as *presence*' (OG 12). But Derrida's concern is emphatically with what is 'enigmatic' about 'presence' (see OG 70), not least insofar as *speech is not the opposite of writing*. What fascinates him is rather the 'strange space . . . *between* speech and writing' and what lies 'beyond the tranquil familiarity' of 'our illusion that they are two' (Diff 5). In fact, as will be obvious to anyone who has listened to him in a seminar, lecture, roundtable discussion or whatever, Derrida loves *talking*. In interview he has indeed confessed to not getting 'a lot of pleasure out of writing' and even to having 'a certain immediate aversion for [it]' (TNON 196). Elsewhere he has said: 'people who are in a bit too much of a hurry have thought that I wasn't interested in the voice, just writing. Obviously, this is not true. What interests me is writing in the voice, the voice as differential vibration' (Dia 140).

The meditation on 'come' that comes at the end of the essay on apocalyptic tone has to do with precisely this notion of 'voice as differential vibration'. 'Come' has sexual connotations in French (*Viens*) as well as in English. Here it is perhaps worth bearing in mind Derrida's characterization of (sexual) bliss (or *jouissance*) as 'differential vibration': 'This "differential vibration" is for me the only possible form of response to desire, the only form of bliss . . . I cannot imagine a living bliss which is not plural, differential' (Dia 137). Here too we might recall the link between coming and the promise, as evoked by Derrida in his essay on Marie-Françoise Plissart's erotic photo-novel *Right of Inspection* (first published in French in 1985): 'Pleasure will have reached its climax, nothing less. Haven't you ever come on a promise? Have you ever enjoyed anything else?' (RI, n.p.). In these respects it is perhaps hardly surprising to find 'come' figure so powerfully and hauntingly in some of the greatest romantic texts in English, such as Shakespeare's *Antony and Cleopatra* (1606–7) or Emily Brontë's *Wuthering Heights* (1847). Consider in Brontë's text, for example, that uncanny moment in which Lockwood witnesses Heathcliff's call to his supposedly dead lover:

> [Heathcliff] got on to the bed and wrenched open the lattice, bursting, as he pulled at it, into an uncontrollable passion of tears.
>
> 'Come in! come in!' he sobbed. 'Cathy, do come. Oh, do – *once* more! Oh! My heart's darling, hear me *this* time . . .!'
>
> (Brontë 1990, 23)

This 'come' haunts the novel (as it haunts the perhaps more nostalgic inflection of the 'come home' in the famous Kate Bush song) from start to finish, or rather, we might say, from before the start. It would be, in effect, where the novel comes from. The novel would be a response to the 'come'.

SHAKESPEARE AND THE EXPERIENCE OF THE IMPOSSIBLE

A study of the word 'come' in Shakespeare would require a separate book; but we can perhaps hear it at work, ecstatically, in the extraordinary affirmations at the ends of the lives of Antony and Cleopatra. 'Come then', says Antony, as he prepares to end himself by running into his sword 'As to a lover's bed' (4.15.101). A few moments earlier he has said: 'I come, my Queen . . . Stay for me./Where souls do couch on flowers we'll hand in hand,/And with our sprightly port make the ghosts gaze.' (4.15.50–2). (The editors of *The Norton Shakespeare* suggest a quite crass 'translation' of the beautiful phrase 'sprightly port' as, simply, 'cheerful stance'. 'Sprightly port' is a phrase on which we could linger a long time, not least because its multiple evocations of the step or gait, the spectral and the affirmative, have such clear affinities with the ghostly 'walking' that can be traced across *Wuthering Heights* as well as with the 'step', 'gait' or 'bearing' of deconstruction remarked on a bit earlier.) And as Cleopatra prepares to kill herself, she declares: 'methinks I hear/Antony call, I see him rouse himself/To praise my noble act [. . .] Husband, I come' (5.2.274–8). As she draws up the poisonous asps in order to kiss them she says: 'So, have you done?/Come then, and take the last warmth of my lips' (5.2.281–2). In every case it is a 'come' for no one, a sprightly, spectral 'come' addressed to no one or to someone who is not only absent from the scene but believed to be dead.

We might note here a fascination that Shakespeare and Derrida evidently share with the motif of 'the impossible' or what Derrida calls, in his essay on *Romeo and Juliet*, 'the theater of the impossible'. When it comes to two lovers, it is a question of 'the duel': the 'absolute certainty . . . is that one must die before the other'. 'It is impossible', says Derrida, 'that we should each survive the other. That's the duel, the axiomatic of every duel, the scene which is the most common and the least spoken of – or the most prohibited – concerning our relation to the other.' Derrida's interest in *Romeo and Juliet* has to do with the fact that here, in this play, 'in the experience of Romeo and Juliet', '*the impossible happens'* (AC 422). *Antony and Cleopatra* is also a play in which 'two people each outlive the other' (422): it presents a certain 'experience of the impossible', to recall one of the definitions of deconstruction noted in the preceding chapter. It is here, perhaps, that we might start to explore some of the intimate links between deconstruction and literature and in particular the crucial idea that deconstruction is not something to be 'applied' to a literary work, like an asp. The poisonous remedy is already to hand, at work, in the work. As Derrida has said, in a nicely aphoristic (or perhaps aspistic) formulation: 'Deconstruction . . . is a coming-to-terms with literature' (Dec 9).

BRONTË AND THE EXPERIENCE OF THE IMPOSSIBLE

A singularly different but also similar 'experience' seems to be at issue in Brontë's *Wuthering Heights*. It comes, perhaps, through the deranging convolutions and retrospectives of narrative time. The novel opens, we may recall, with Lockwood's recalling in the *present* tense his immediate impressions of 'hav[ing] just returned' from meeting Heathcliff for the first time, but this 'same' narrative ends with Lockwood recalling in the *past* tense his visit to Heathcliff's grave with its 'still bare' headstone (Brontë 3, 256). If Brontë's novel figures the experience of the impossible, this would have to do with the intricately deranging repetitions of narrative structure and doublings of names (the splitting of the text at its heart, the death of one Catherine coinciding with the birth of another), and above all with the sense of Catherine and Heathcliff as ghosts or revenants (literally, 'those who come back'), living on, and outliving one another. Already from the very 'beginning' (which is thus haunted and not a beginning, like each and every beginning, in Derrida's terms), Heathcliff is a kind of ghost. He is a ghost in light of the eerie temporal perspective or perspectivism that the novel generates. (To read this novel is to participate in what J. Hillis Miller calls 'a multiple act of resurrection, an opening of graves [and] a raising of ghosts': see Brontë 392; Miller 1982, 71.) Heathcliff is a ghost in light of the fact that his very name is a revenant ('it was the name of a son who had died in childhood' [29]). He is a ghost in the sense that, after his death and burial, 'country folks . . . would swear on their Bible that he *walks*' (255).

Overhearing that Cathy proposes to marry another man, Edgar Linton, Heathcliff disappears for several years. No one seems to know where he came *from*, and now he has apparently vanished off the face of the earth again. As if he is dead, however, he comes back. With a face suggesting not so much 'gladness' as 'an awful calamity', Catherine tells her husband Edgar: 'Heathcliff's come back – he is!' (73). One lover outlives the other. Heathcliff outlives Catherine who had already apparently outlived him. In the feverish delirium of her 'insanity', approaching her death, Catherine knows that it is an issue of coming, of asking ghosts to come, and of being a ghost oneself. She throws open the window of her room at Thrushcross Grange and looks out into the 'misty darkness' across the moors towards the house where she believes Heathcliff to be. Her 'ravings' are mentally transcribed, recorded and brought back to life by the witness-narrator Nelly Dean. In this respect we can note already the disruptive effect, in Brontë's novel, of what Derrida calls 'writing in the voice' and indeed of a 'differential vibration'. The 'call to come', as Derrida puts it elsewhere, 'happens only in multiple voices' (PIO 62).

Such is the insane scenario of narration in which all of this is happening: it is a delirium of voices in which Nelly Dean's voice transmits the voice of the dead Catherine in the writing of Lockwood's diary in the strangely absent, spectrally surviving 'authorial voice' of Emily Brontë. Catherine's ravings involve the delusion of having 'caught [the] shining' of candlelight in the window of the servant Joseph's garret at Wuthering Heights:

'Look!' she cried eagerly. '. . . Joseph sits up late, doesn't he? He's waiting till I come home that he may lock the gate. Well, he'll wait a while yet. It's a rough journey, and a sad heart to travel it; and we must pass by Gimmerton Kirk, to go that journey! We've braved its ghosts often together, and dared each other to stand among the graves and ask them to come. But Heathcliff, if I dare you now, will you venture? If you do, I'll keep you. I'll not lie there by myself; they may bury me twelve feet deep, and throw the church down over me, but I won't rest till you are with me. I never will!'

She paused, and resumed with a strange smile, 'He's considering – he'd rather I'd come to him! Find a way, then! Not through that Kirkyard.'

(Brontë 98)

Brontë's text plays – and this is a play of the most serious kind, a play that involves that sense of 'give' I was talking about earlier on. It is a play that does not require any centring in the intention of the author or of the character, a play or freedom that 'belongs' to the structure of language rather than, and indeed prior to, the agency of any writing or speaking subject. In particular here we could say that the text plays on the etymology of 'venture', from the Latin verb *venīre*, to come. To venture is to come, perhaps, but first of all it is to dare, to dare to go or come, to take risks. To venture is inextricably bound up with a sense of hazard (one of the archaic senses of 'venture' is 'hazard' or 'chance') and of the performative. To challenge or dare, we may recall from our earlier discussion, is an example of a so-called performative speech act. 'But Heathcliff, if I dare you now, will you venture?' Catherine's speech itself ventures, it ventures itself as a kind of mad performative: are you coming to me or would you rather I come to you? The addressee of this dare is not, apparently, present: it is a spectral performative, a performative in the dark, without a home.

It is mad also, however, on account of the pause, the resumption and 'strange smile' in which we are invited to consider Catherine considering Heathcliff considering 'he'd rather I'd come to him!' 'Come': what does this mean? How should we read or hear this word? Find a way, the text seems to venture, that does not go by the way of ghosts, knowing all along that there is no 'come', no 'coming' without ghosts, for the text itself is a ghost, it is the coming of ghosts *en masse*. As Derrida has remarked: 'It must be possible to *summon* a spectre, to appeal to it for example . . . there may be something of the revenant, of the return, at the origin or the conclusion of every "come hither"' (DA 535). The madness of this passage in *Wuthering Heights* is in part that of what we would call telepathy: Catherine's 'strange smile' is apparently knowing. She can apparently 'hear' what he is thinking or desiring, requesting or ordering: it turns on a 'come', without our being able to tell where this 'come' comes from, without our being able to tell whether it is a desire or an order for example, indeed without our being able to tell whether it is (in Derrida's words) 'a citation in the current sense' (AT 65). But this 'experience of the impossible' (the telepathic 'come') is what the novel is about. The impossible, as we know, happens. 'Come in! come in!' he sobbed. 'Cathy, do come. Oh, do – *once* more! Oh! My heart's darling, hear me *this* time . . .!' (23) 'Do come', come '*once* more': where will this 'come' have come from and where rest?

COME SPOOKED

In both *Wuthering Heights* and *Antony and Cleopatra*, there appears to be a sort of ghost-writing or spectrography of the 'come'. One 'come' calls the other, there is the call of the other to come apparently in the knowledge of the death of the other, a 'come' that is at least double-voiced, a sort of differential, disembodied 'come' the source of which is no more the lips of Heathcliff than those of Catherine (or, in Shakespeare's play, no more the lips of Cleopatra than those of Antony). There is rather, perhaps, what Derrida describes as 'a spectrography of tone and of change of tone [that] could not by definition keep itself at the disposal of or to the measure of the philosophical, pedagogical or teaching demonstration' (AT 64). In their singular effects of multiple voice and difference-within-the-voice (which I have been trying to evoke here through notions of spectrality and sprightliness, narratorial delirium and telepathy), these literary works perhaps give us to hear something of what Derrida is getting at, or trying to get to come, in the final pages of his essay on apocalyptic tone.

'Come' is affirmative, says Derrida:

> In this *affirmative* tone, 'Come' marks in itself, in oneself, neither a desire nor an order, neither a prayer nor a request. More precisely, the grammatical, linguistic, or semantic categories from which the 'Come' would thus be determined are traversed by the 'Come'.
>
> (AT 65)

This 'Come' would be what 'precedes and calls the event', it would be 'that starting from which there is any event' (64). It is apocalyptic while announcing 'the apocalypse of apocalypse' (66). 'Plural in itself' and 'in oneself', 'Come' 'addresses without message and without destination' (66). This ghostly 'come' has as much to do with desire as terror, as much to do with bliss as with death. It resists categorization, it is not to be placed. As Derrida puts it:

> ['Come' is] less 'anterior' to any order or any desire in itself – since it is at once an order and a desire, a demand, etc. – than 'anterior' to all logical and grammatical *categories* of order, of desire as these have come to be determined in Western grammar or logic and which permit us to say: 'come' [belongs to one or another of] these categories . . . 'Come' resists this categorization. This does not mean it is foreign to desire or to order; it is desire, order, injunction,

demand, need, but these are categories, derived conceptual oppositions without pertinence as regards the 'come'.

(Dia 150)

What the 'come' in Derrida perhaps most breathtakingly evokes is the sense that, as he puts it in an interview in 1983, 'everything remains open, still to be thought'. It has to do with what can 'cause to tremble a very simple sentence, a word, a timbre of voice' (U 131): be free. Be free, free of being, come 'beyond being' (AT 65), 'incomparably beyond', as Cathy says in another passage about 'coming' in *Wuthering Heights* (see Brontë 124). 'Come', as evoked in the essay on apocalyptic tone, corresponds with what Derrida elsewhere says about 'yes'. In an essay on James Joyce's *Ulysses* (1922), he talks about 'the question of the *yes*' as 'mobiliz[ing] or travers[ing] everything [he has] been trying to think, write, teach, or read' (UG 287). Yes, be free: in that essay Derrida provides an extensive analysis of the 'differential vibration' (UG 305) of the 'yes' in Joyce, elaborating the notion of a yes that, like the 'come', is an affirmation, a *yes* 'more "ancient" than the question "what is?" . . . a *yes* more ancient than knowledge' (UG 296).

POLITICS AND LITERATURE

I would like to conclude with a couple of brief remarks concerning politics and literature. In this chapter I have attempted to explore what perhaps links these two topics or questions. Derrida's work is impelled by a passionate commitment to what he calls the democracy to come: despite the platitudes of so many politicians, democracy is always a promise. There is never a point at which it has fully finally arrived. This was, for Derrida, the terrible mistake of Marxism, or at least of a certain Marxism (for Derrida does not simply dissociate himself from Marxism, on the contrary his book *Specters of Marx* is a new call for a 'new international'; he affirms 'the necessity for a new culture, one that would invent another way of reading and analysing *Capital*, both Marx's book and capital in general' [OH 56]). For Derrida, Marxism's error entailed 'the animist incorporation of an emancipatory eschatology which ought to have respected the promise, the being-promise of a promise' (SM 105). The promise that Derrida identifies with democracy and with justice is a commitment to a future that is 'beyond every present life, beyond every living being who can already say "me, now"' (DA 546).

It is an 'endless promise' (TSICL 38). (I discuss the links between deconstruction, democracy and justice at greater length in Chapter 9.)

This promise of a democracy to come is intimately entwined with the experience of the yes, the 'rebellious force of affirmation', the 'be free', the 'come'. It is also, as I have been trying to make clear, intimately engaged with questions of literature, in particular with regard to the 'experience of the impossible'. The 'strange institution called literature' (in Derrida's phrase: see TSICL) is bound up with the law and with freedom: be free. As he has remarked: 'The possibility of literature, the legitimation that a society gives it, the allaying of suspicion or terror with regard to it, all that goes together – politically – with the unlimited right to ask any question, to suspect all dogmatism, to analyse every presupposition, even those of the ethics or the politics of responsibility' (POO 23). Literature is inextricably linked to principles of 'freedom of speech' and 'freedom of thought' (cf. OH 50). As Salman Rushdie has put it: 'Literature is the one place in any society where, within the secrecy of our own heads, we can hear *voices talking about everything in every possible way*' (Rushdie 1991, 429). This possibility of being free, free to say anything and everything, is (as Rushdie perhaps knows better than many other people) bound up with transgression, with a capacity, tendency, or desire to 'defy' or 'break free of the rules' (see TSICL 36–7). Derrida has described this as follows:

> The institution of literature in the West, in its relatively modern form, is linked to an authorization to say everything, and doubtless too to the coming about of the modern idea of democracy. Not that it depends on a democracy in place, but it seems inseparable to me from what calls forth a democracy, in the most open (and doubtless itself to come) sense of democracy.
>
> (TSICL 37)

Rushdie characterizes literature as a 'place'. I am not sure about this. It might be more exact to consider literature as a certain experience of displacement, a questioning of any and every sense of 'place'. This is what I have been trying to evoke in relation to the 'come', a 'come' that has no 'origin', no identifiable 'sender or decidable addressee' (AT 66). Literature has no definitive meaning or resting place, even if it allows one to explore notions of 'definitive meaning' and 'resting place' in especially critical and productive ways. The literary work never rests. It does not belong. Literature does not come home: it is strangely homeless, strangely free.

5

SUPPLEMENT

No key ideas in Derrida, then, or nothing but key ideas: that was one of our starting points. This paradox might be most neatly illustrated in the notion of the supplement. It is apparent in everything he writes, but the most succinct treatment comes in his remarkable reading of the work of Jean-Jacques Rousseau, in particular in a chapter of *Of Grammatology* (1967) entitled ' ". . . That Dangerous Supplement . . ."' (OG 141–64). In the following pages I shall focus on this section of *Of Grammatology* in order to provide an introductory account of the notion of the supplement and suggest some of the ways the supplement is at work in literature and elsewhere.

THREE DOTS

The so-called 'original' French title of the chapter in *Of Grammatology* is ' "ce dangereux supplément . . ."': there is a good case for translating it as ' "this dangerous supplement . . ."' . The 'that' puts the supplement over there, at a distance. The 'this' brings it closer to home, where it really belongs in all its strangeness and un-belonging: the supplement is right here, in this very sentence, in this very phrase. The title-phrase, 'that dangerous supplement', is also of course in quotation marks: it occurs in the writings of Rousseau. Again, the form of the title offers some advance warning as to the curious character of the supplement 'itself': Derrida's essay supplies itself with a title from someone else, from another text or texts. In ways that I hope will become clearer as we go on, a title is always a kind of supplement.

Then there is the seemingly small matter of the three dots . . . In the French version there are three dots at the end of the title ('"ce dangereux supplément . . ."'). In the English translation there are three dots at the beginning as well ('". . . That Dangerous Supplement . . ."'). In adding three dots (or an ellipsis) at the beginning of the phrase, the English translator, Gayatri Chakravorty Spivak, supplements the French text. In this way she effectively points up what the less flamboyant French version already suggests, namely the fact that this text, this essay called '". . . That Dangerous Supplement . . ."' is part of a larger text, that there is something before it (something that it is supplementing) as well as something after it (by which it could or should be supplemented). Spivak's translation (at once faithful and violating) thus emphasizes the fact that the significance or readability of an ellipsis depends on context but at the same time also on broaching the question of the borders of a discourse or text.

This uncertainty is evident in the ambiguity or, perhaps, undecidability inscribed in the double sense of 'ellipsis' (or 'three dots') as conventionally defined. An ellipsis, the dictionary tells us, is 'a figure of syntax by which a word or words are left out and merely implied (*grammar*); mark(s) indicating ellipsis (*printing*)' (*Chambers Dictionary*). The word 'ellipsis' involves what Derrida has in another context called 'an *elliptical* essence' (Ell 296): is the word (or are the words) 'left out' or not? Is what is 'left out' the same as what is 'merely implied'? How can what is 'left out' at the same time be a 'mark' or 'marks'? What *is* an ellipsis or 'three dots'? In some respects perhaps Derrida's most famous single essay or book-extract, ' ". . . That Dangerous Supplement . . ."' is among other things a profound meditation on the importance and effects of three dots. Three dots (a strangely singular and plural noun) always signify a logic of the supplement.

WHAT IS A SUPPLEMENT?

A supplement is at once what is added on to something in order further to enrich it *and* what is added on as a mere 'extra' (from the Latin for 'outside'). It is both 'a surplus, a plenitude enriching another plenitude', *and* it makes up for something missing, as if there is a void to be filled up: 'it is not simply added to the positivity of a presence . . . its place is assigned in the structure by the mark of an emptiness' (OG 144–5). Derrida explores the strange but necessary 'cohabitation' (144) of these two significations of the supplement. In both cases the supplement is conceived as exterior, as an 'extra'. Yet the supplement entails a kind of crazy logic: it is neither inside nor outside, and/or both inside and outside at the same time. It forms part without being part, it belongs without belonging. As Derrida puts it: 'The supplement is maddening, because it is neither presence nor absence' (154).

In his reading of Rousseau in ' ". . . That Dangerous Supplement . . ."' Derrida describes and transforms what we might understand by the word 'supplement'. The notion of a supplement may seem very familiar: we might think, for example, of the newspaper supplement or the supplement to a dictionary or a postscript to a letter. It is characteristic of Derrida's work in this respect that he painstakingly effaces any such familiarity, defamiliarizes what seemed 'normal', producing a radical transformation or 'deformation' of what we might have thought was the 'original' concept under discussion. He describes this strategy very well in his thesis defence in 1980:

> Every conceptual breakthrough amounts to transforming, that is to say deforming, an accredited, authorized relationship between a word and a concept, between a trope and what one had every interest to consider to be an unshiftable primary sense, a proper, literal or current usage.
>
> (TTP 40–1)

It is possible to see this strategy – what he elsewhere calls a 'strange strategy without finality' (O 7) – operating in innumerable other contexts: for example, in relation to 'text', 'trace', 'writing', 'pharmakon', 'hymen' and so on. Every such 'conceptual breakthrough' broaches what he calls an 'unbounded generalization' (TTP 40).

The supplement turns out to have been everywhere or rather, everywhere and nowhere, since, as Derrida emphasizes, the supplement in a sense 'is nothing' (OG 244). As he puts it in the closing pages of Of Grammatology:

> It is the strange essence of the supplement not to have essentiality: it may always not have taken place. Moreover, literally, it has never taken place: it is never present, here and now. If it were, it would not be what it is, a supplement.

> . . . Less than nothing and yet, to judge by its effects, much more than nothing.
> The supplement is neither a presence nor an absence. No ontology can think
> its operation.
>
> (OG 314)

The supplement cannot be thought under the rubric of an ontology, in other words of a philosophy focused on the concept of being (*ontos* in ancient Greek). Rather, it would be a question of what, in a later text, *Specters of Marx* (1993), Derrida calls a 'hauntology' (SM 10). The supplement haunts. It is ghostly. To describe the effects of what leaves its trace without ever itself being either present or absent and thereby to transform the terrain: this would be a way of construing deconstruction. We can never be done with the 'effects' of the supplement, not least because it is (as Derrida notes, in a phrase taken from Rousseau's *Confessions*) 'almost inconceivable to reason' (OG 149). To which Derrida adds: 'simple irrationality, the opposite of reason, are less irritating and waylaying for classical logic' (OG 154). That is what is so 'maddening' about it.

The supplement is like a virus. It infects everything. 'The virulence of this concept', Derrida declares, is such that it is impossible 'to *arrest* it, domesticate it, tame it' (OG 157). The word 'virulence' comes to us from the Latin *vīrus*, 'venom' or 'poison'. This extraordinary virulence of the supplement is the very logic of the virus: it adds itself on, it is a supplement. As Derrida says elsewhere: 'the virus will have been the only object of my work' (C 91–2). (For a compelling elaboration of the viral nature of deconstruction specifically in relation to AIDS, see Düttmann 1996.) It is perhaps easier to witness the strangeness of the workings of this virus in the so-called 'original' French texts of Rousseau and Derrida, where there is a shifting between the supplement or supplementary (*supplément*, *supplémentaire*) and the substitute (*suppléant*) or 'substitutive supplementation' (*suppléance*). The verb *suppléer* in French is 'To add what is missing, to supply a necessary surplus': this is the definition Derrida elsewhere cites as an example of the dictionary (in this case Littré) 'respecting, like a sleepwalker, the strange logic of this word' (see FSW 212).

In English 'to supplement' is an obsolete sense of the verb 'to supply' (one of Derrida's key ideas, if you like, will have been to rethink 'obsolete sense'), but this overlap is evident in various respects in so-called 'current English' as well. The verb 'to supply' means 'to fill,

occupy (as a substitute)' (*Chambers Dictionary*) – as in 'to supply the missing words . . .' (three dots, again). The link between supplement and
substitute is especially evident in the phrase 'supply teacher' (in British
English) or 'substitute teacher' (in the US). This educational context is
perhaps not simply fortuitous. It is part of Derrida's argument that, for
Rousseau, 'all education . . . [is] described or presented as a system of
substitution [*suppléance*]' (OG 145): all education is 'originally' supply
or substitute education. In Rousseau's writing, education is consistently
figured as standing in for – and making up for – 'Nature'. 'Nature' itself,
for Rousseau, 'does not supplement *itself* at all' (145). For Derrida,
however, there is nothing *before* the logic of the supplement, or as he
puts it elsewhere in *Of Grammatology*: 'One wishes to go back *from the
supplement to the source*: one must recognize that there is *a supplement at
the source*' (OG 304). All of Derrida's work might be encapsulated within
a notion of supply or substitute teaching, a teaching of the supplement.

SPEECH AND WRITING

My account of Derrida's account of Rousseau can hardly substitute for
the real thing. If you read ' ". . . That Dangerous Supplement . . ."' you
can perhaps experience for yourself something of the uncanny strangeness that Derrida's meticulous reading brings out. Citing and reciting,
linking and analysing the many moments where Rousseau writes about
notions of supplement, supplying and substitution, Derrida makes him
a kind of stranger to himself. Is the 'real thing' in Derrida's account
or already in Rousseau? Derrida ranges across numerous Rousseau
texts, from *Emile* (1762) and *The Confessions* (completed in 1765, first
published in 1781) to far lesser known writings such as the short piece
posthumously published under the title 'Pronunciation' (see AL 83,
n. 6). He explores the consistency with which Rousseau's texts rely on
the notion of supplement, perhaps most decisively in relation to writing
and to masturbation. Derrida quotes what is in some respects perhaps
a very familiar-looking, commonsensical statement from Rousseau:

> Languages are made to be spoken, writing serves only as a supplement to
> speech ... Speech represents thought by conventional signs, and writing
> represents the same with regard to speech. Thus the art of writing is nothing
> but a mediated representation of thought.
>
> ('Pronunciation', cited in OG 144)

Derrida picks up the scent of danger here and describes it as follows:

> Writing is dangerous from the moment that representation there claims to be presence and the sign of the thing itself. And there is a fatal necessity, inscribed in the very functioning of the sign, that the substitute make one forget the vicariousness of its own function and make itself pass for the plenitude of a speech whose deficiency and infirmity it nevertheless only *supplements*.
>
> (OG 144)

This is not to say that Rousseau simply mistrusts writing. On the contrary, as Derrida makes clear, he 'valorizes and disqualifies writing at the same time . . . Rousseau condemns writing as destruction of presence and as disease of speech. He rehabilitates it to the extent that it promises the reappropriation of that of which speech allowed itself to be dispossessed' (141–2).

Derrida sees these as two forms of desire on Rousseau's part: the condemnation and disqualification of writing belong to his 'theory of language', the valorization and rehabilitation to his 'experience [as a] writer' (142). In order to be 'true to nature' (to recall a phrase from the opening sentences of *The Confessions*) Rousseau must be absent in order to write. Derrida quotes Jean Starobinski quoting *The Confessions*:

> I would love society like others, if I were not sure of showing myself not only at a disadvantage, but as completely different from what I am. The part that I have taken of *writing and hiding myself* is precisely the one that suits me. If I were present, one would never know what I was worth.
>
> (cited in OG 142)

Writing is merely 'a supplement to speech' (in Rousseau's phrase), it is characterized by absence and secondariness; and yet it can also be seen to work the other way around. There is a kind of primacy, presence and 'worth' that writing can embody, that is not possible in 'society'. By hiding, by making himself absent Rousseau aims, in and through writing, at what Derrida calls 'the greatest symbolic reappropriation of presence' (143).

What is perhaps most extraordinary about Derrida's account concerns the movement of 'unbounded generalization' that I mentioned earlier. 'Writing' as supplement is transformed: it is no longer that which can simply be opposed to speech, nor 'merely' is it a supplement to speech. As the possibility of being able to produce meanings even when the writer (or speaker) is dead, 'writing' takes on an uncanny new significance: with this word, 'writing', Derrida provisionally names something that is not linguistic or discursive, even as it makes language or discourse possible. What is at issue here is the importance of recognizing that, while Derrida's work is deeply concerned with the nature of 'writing' in its traditional (alphabetic, Western sense) – stressing its place, for example, as what 'opens the field of history' (OG 27) – he is at the same time just as or even more deeply concerned with a thinking of writing as non-alphabetic, other-than-Western, pre-linguistic, indeed as something that is not unique to humans at all. Let us move towards a clarification of this difficult business with what may appear a digression upon the nature of masturbation.

MASTURBATION

It is still a question of the supplement or of what we might call 'supplementing nature'. Speech is natural, writing supplements nature; sex is natural, masturbation supplements nature. But nature will always already have been supplemented: this is (in) the nature of the supplement. As the contemporary critic and theorist Leo Bersani asks: 'Who are you when you masturbate?' (Bersani 1995, 103). Answer: in what Bersani calls 'fantasy' (103) or Derrida calls 'the imaginary' (OG 151). As the latter writes:

> Rousseau will never stop having recourse to, and accusing himself of, this onanism that permits one to affect oneself by providing oneself with presences, by summoning absent beauties. In his eyes it will remain the model of vice and perversion. Affecting oneself by another presence, one *corrupts* oneself [makes oneself other] by oneself [*on s'altère soi-même*]. Rousseau neither wishes to think nor can think that this alteration does not simply happen to the self, that it is the self's very origin.
>
> (OG 153, translation slightly modified)

Onanism, masturbation or what our forefathers (if not our foremothers) liked to call self-abuse may belong to the realms of fantasy or the imaginary, but this doesn't mean we are not dealing here with the so-called real world. On the contrary, our very sense of 'self' and 'world' is at stake here. Masturbation is a strange thing. It is what Rousseau variously calls a 'dangerous supplement' and a 'fatal advantage' (quoted in OG 150–1). As the contemporary critic and theorist Barbara Johnson has commented: masturbation is 'both a symbolic form of ideal union, since in it the subject and object are truly one, and a radical alienation of the self from any contact with an other' (see D xii).

'Affecting oneself' is what Derrida elsewhere talks about as auto-affection: 'auto-affection' brings together what in different contexts are known as 'self-presence' and 'narcissism'. The purest form of auto-affection is 'hearing oneself speak' (SP 79). Derrida's account of this topic consists in a very detailed critical engagement with phenomenological discourse and thinking, especially that of Edmund Husserl. (To follow up on deconstruction and phenomenology, see in particular, *Edmund Husserl's 'Origin of Geometry': An Introduction* (1962, revised edition 1974) [OGI], *Speech and Phenomena* (1967) [SP] and *Of Grammatology* [OG].) Hearing oneself speak – that is to say, even if one is keeping silent, listening to oneself in the interiority of one's own head, keeping an ear out, so to speak, in order to be able to hear oneself think – hearing oneself speak is perhaps the most natural thing in the world. If it is 'the most natural thing in the world', we also know, or think we know, that hearing oneself speak is not 'really' in the world at all: we like to think and feel that it doesn't involve having to 'pass through what is outside the sphere of "ownness"' (SP 78) in any way. But as anyone who has heard their voice on a tape also 'knows', things are not so simple or so sweet. I don't believe I am entirely alone in feeling that the experience of 'really' hearing oneself speak is very often a horrible one. 'Is that really me? I don't sound like that! It must be the tape. That's awful, it's ghastly, how nauseating.' And so on.

In *Of Grammatology*, in *Speech and Phenomena*, and in the superb essay 'Qual Quelle' (1971) (QQ), for example, Derrida argues that hearing oneself speak is not the immediate, unmediated, spontaneous affair we may like to suppose it is. Whatever form of auto-affection we are dealing with, there is always a logic of the supplement, a work of supplementation and substitution going on. In the beginning was the supplement. It is a matter of what Derrida calls 'the supplement of origin' (see SP 87 ff). 'Immediacy is derived', as *Of Grammatology* has it: thus it becomes necessary to speak of 'the *mirage* of the thing itself, of immediate presence, of originary perception' (OG 157, my emphasis). In 'Qual Quelle', Derrida proposes that the poet Paul Valéry (1871–1945) understands the strangeness of 'hearing oneself speak' better than

Husserl or Hegel or indeed 'any traditional philosopher' (QQ 287). If one is looking for the source of the voice one has to reckon with the fact that (as Valéry puts it) '[t]he origin . . . is imaginary' (quoted in QQ 297, n. 25). We might then suppose that poetry, at least as clearly as philosophy, provides us with a sense of this strange supplementarity, and later on in this book I will try to explore this through a reading of Coleridge's *Kubla Khan*. The 'mirage' that Derrida speaks about has its counterpart in the essay on Valéry: we are all living, Derrida suggests, under 'a "regime" of normal hallucination' (QQ 297). As he puts it: 'To hear oneself is the most normal and the most impossible experience' (QQ 297). We could say that all of Derrida's work is impelled by this kind of desire to experience the impossible '*in [his] body*' (Ja 49). And we might wish to recall in this context what he has called 'the least bad definition' of deconstruction, that is to say a certain 'experience of the impossible' (Aft 200).

Now what I have just been talking about might appear as a digression. Hearing oneself speak is not exactly the same thing as masturbation. But Derrida's reading of Rousseau does, among other things, prompt a rethinking of the 'nature' of masturbation. Derrida declares: '[s]exual auto-affection, that is auto-affection in general, neither begins nor ends with what one thinks can be circumscribed by the name of masturbation' (OG 154–5). There is, Derrida suggests, more to life – more to auto-affection or the ability to be affected – than this 'dangerous supplement'. At the same time, he leaves open the question of the limits of what 'masturbation' names, of how this name can or should be circumscribed. What is the relationship between masturbation and the literary? Or indeed between masturbation and what Derrida, apropos of James Joyce's *Ulysses*, calls 'mental telephony' (UG 272)? There are of course the ostensibly straightforward cases of what Rousseau refers to as 'those dangerous books which a fine lady finds inconvenient because, she says, they can only be read with one hand' (OG 340, n.8). But Derrida's caution suggests that masturbation may have a more complex significance, especially in the context of the question of that 'imaginary' world called literature. I leave this for you to ruminate on further. You may wish to contemplate your novels – or at least novels such as those of Thomas Hardy and John Fowles. It is in the context of a discussion of Hardy's *The Well-Beloved* (1898) (his strangely beautiful, neglected final novel, about the figure of the beloved as always conforming to a logic of the supplement), that the novelist John Fowles declares what he calls the 'simple truth', namely that 'novel writing is an onanistic and taboo-laden pursuit' (Fowles 1999, 160).

GHOSTLY CONCLUSION

I would like to bring this discussion of the notion of the supplement to a conclusion, but of course I can't. The logic of the supplement entails the disruption of what we think we understand by 'the end', as much as 'the beginning'. Neither present nor absent, it is ghostly, maddening, something that you can't finish with. Permit me, however, at least to offer a brief outline of a few of the ways in which Derrida's thinking on the supplement might have a more general relevance for thinking about approaching literary or philosophical texts, or of course about other so-called 'media', such as film. (There is no representation or recording, no channel or transmission without the interruption and interference of a logic of supplementarity. That, in part, is why Derrida characterizes TV, radio and tape-recordings, the internet, film and video as ghostly. For more on this see, for example, his book with Bernard Stiegler, *Echographies of Television* (ET), or the film *Ghostdance* (director, Ken McMullen, 1983).)

A series of five supplementary remarks, then, about the pertinence of the supplementary. Each of these remarks supplements, spills over into, stands in for each of the others:

1   In '". . . That Dangerous Supplement . . ."', Derrida argues that blindness to the supplement is the law of the writer. He contends that '[t]he concept of the supplement is a sort of blind spot in Rousseau's text' (OG 163). The specific strangeness of the supplement that Derrida's reading explores is something that is and is not articulated in Rousseau's writings: this is not so much a matter of one-upmanship on Derrida's part, but rather of trying to reckon with the notion that, as he emphatically puts it: *'blindness to the supplement* is the law' (OG 149). Derrida's concern is thus with the supplementary logic whereby an author (Jean-Jacques Rousseau but also Jacques Derrida, you and I) can always say 'more, less, or something other than what he *would mean* [or would want to say: *voudrait dire*]' (OG 158). Derrida is not uninterested in 'authorial intention': on the contrary, he argues that trying to take it into account is a crucial element in any critical reading. But the logic

of the supplement dictates (in a perhaps rather eerie sense of 'dictation') that the writer is always susceptible to being taken by surprise. A writer can never have complete command or mastery over what s/he writes. Neither can a reader. What Derrida calls 'critical reading' entails the attempt to do justice to this 'exorbitance', to '*produce*' (158, his emphasis) the effects of this strange logic.

2   Derrida's attention to the notion of the supplement encourages us to think more carefully about what might be called the supplement in its allegedly 'normal', 'conventional' sense. Here we could consider how the notion of the supplement is at work in the context of all sorts of peritexts, such as prefaces, introductions, forewords, afterwords, dedications, acknowledgements, epilogues, postscripts, footnotes, appendices, parentheses and digressions. Reflecting on the strangeness of the supplement, of supplementarity and substitution, inevitably leads to a rethinking of what we might formerly have supposed was the *non*-supplementary. In this respect it is no doubt not by chance that Derrida's work has from the very beginning been characterized by a willingness and indeed a compulsion to explore the apparently 'minor' elements of a writer's work, whether in the form of texts (such as Rousseau's 'Essay on the Origin of Languages' in *Of Grammatology*) considered superfluous or supplementary to the canonical works by that author (*The Confessions* or *Emile*) or in the form of prefaces, footnotes or other seemingly superfluous or supplementary elements within the so-called 'main body' of a writer's work. (The most celebrated example here would be Derrida's '*Ousia* and *Grammē*' [O&G], a 35-page 'note on a note' from Heidegger's *Being and Time* (1927).) This of course is another reason why the notion of 'key ideas' is so misleading in the context of getting a sense of what Derrida's work is about as well as a sense of what the works he reads are about.

3   More than once in this chapter I have felt obliged to use quotation marks when referring to Derrida's and Rousseau's 'original' French texts. In an apparently commonsensical way, we may think of the French text as being the original and of the English translation as being secondary. Derrida argues, however, that a translation is not secondary but is rather a *condition* of the original. Following the celebrated essay 'The Task of the Translator', by the German Jewish writer Walter Benjamin (1892–1940), Derrida proposes

that to be the 'original' the text must be translatable: 'the structure of the original is marked by the requirement to be translated'
(DTB 184). 'Translation augments and modifies the original' (EO
122), as he puts it elsewhere. This 'modifying' work of translation
is at once supplementary and essential.

4   The supplement provides a way of thinking about critical discourse
or metalanguage (i.e. a language used to discuss another language).
Literary criticism and theory, for example, are clearly in some
respects supplementary to their so-called object, the literary work.
We talk about the primary text (the novel, the poem, or whatever)
and the secondary text (the critical essay, monograph or whatever),
but this distinction between primary and secondary is turned upside
down, fundamentally disturbed by a thinking of the supplement.
We all rely on metalanguage, on the notion that there can be a
language on or about another language. Metalanguage is in operation everywhere, from the realm of critical writing in general (all
critical writing is supposedly metalinguistic, a metadiscourse on or
about its literary 'object') to the micrological example such as this
sentence. To refer to 'this sentence' *in the very course of that sentence*
is a metalinguistic gesture, a deictic (as it is known in linguistics)
that takes the language of that sentence as its putative object.
Everyday life would be impossible without metalanguage. But the
notion of metalanguage entails a logic of the supplement. There is
something 'maddening' about the notion: metalanguage is, in short,
both necessary and impossible. We cannot do without it, but there
is no metalanguage as a discrete language: it is both part of and
not part of its so-called object language. We might consider an
everyday example such as an argument in which one person says to
the other, in exasperation: 'I can't believe we're having this conversation!' This statement of disbelief is both part and not part of the
conversation. In a similar (if altogether grander) fashion, Derrida's
reading of Rousseau is inconceivable without Rousseau's text:
his account of Rousseau's writings cannot be straightforwardly
separated off from those writings. Metalanguage is a parasitism,
inseparable from a logic of contamination. But this parasitism and
contamination, this virulence (to recall Derrida's use of this word
earlier) affects both 'language' and 'metalanguage'. To deconstruct
a text is to attempt to take into account the ways in which metalanguage is both necessary and impossible. It entails what Derrida

has called a sort of 'radical metalinguistics', a metalinguistics that 'integrates within itself . . . the impossibility of a metalanguage' (SST 76). (I return to the question of metalanguage, specifically in the context of literature, in Chapter 8.)

5 The supplement is, as Derrida suggests, 'the self's very origin' (OG 153). The self, ego or 'I' is always already caught up in the movement of supplementarity. As he puts it in *Monolingualism of the Other* (1996), the *I* would have to be figured as occupying 'the site of a *situation* that cannot be found, a site always referring elsewhere, to something other, to another language, to the other in general' (MO 29). There is always 'a secret of "me" for "me"' (Dia 134), as he has said in an interview. This is one reason why, he argues, it is so 'foolish' to go on and on about 'problems of *identity*' (MO 10), as if these were essentially resolvable. There is, for Derrida, no identity without a '*disorder of identity*' (MO 14). In *Monolingualism of the Other* in particular, Derrida's concern is to argue that 'an identity is never given, received, or attained; only the interminable and indefinitely phantasmatic process of identification endures' (MO 28). Or as he puts it, more pithily, elsewhere: 'there is no identity. There is identification' (TS 28). Identification is inextricably and interminably bound up with supplementarity, the phantasmatic or imaginary. Identifying always entails a logic of adding on, making up, being in place of. This in turn relates to an affirmation that is at the heart of deconstruction. As Derrida puts it in an essay entitled 'Psyche: Inventions of the Other' (originally given as two lectures in 1984), 'we are (always) (still) to be invented' (PIO 61).

6

TEXT

If the supplement can be said to constitute one of Derrida's 'key ideas', it would be to the extent that it figures an unsettling of borders, a troubling of inside/outside distinctions, a logic of leakage, underflow and overflow, in other words the destabilization of any 'key idea'. In the following pages I shall attempt to show how this is also true for the concept of 'text'. Derrida elaborates the concept of the supplement through a sharply focused reading of Rousseau, but the 'strange economy of the supplement' (OG 154) that his account brings into focus has a pertinence to all sorts of other contexts. His reading thus conforms to a proposition he makes elsewhere (and implicitly *everywhere else* in his writings): 'No meaning can be determined out of context, but no context permits saturation' (LO 81). Derrida always begins (wherever he happens to find himself) in a specific context, which is to say in trying to engage with a specific text or scene of reading. To say this is perhaps inevitably to court the misunderstanding that Derrida is a 'textualist critic', a 'linguistic philosopher' or a 'linguisticist thinker'. I'm sorry if these sound like rather horrible phrases: they are not of my choosing. I will now try to explain, as briefly as I can, why they are also misguided and misleading.

THERE IS NOTHING OUTSIDE THE TEXT

'". . . That Dangerous Supplement . . ."' (OG 141–64) contains perhaps the most famous remark Derrida has ever made. '*There is nothing outside the text*' (*il n'y a pas de hors-texte*) (OG 158), he asserts, and he underlines these words just in case their apparent enormity might be missed: this, he contends, is 'the axial proposition of [the] essay' (163). Along with the word 'deconstruction', this six-word sentence has also been and will perhaps continue to be a source of crucial misunderstandings. As Derrida observes in a 1994 interview with Maurizio Ferraris:

> The first step for me, in the approach to what I proposed to call deconstruction, was a putting into question of the authority of linguistics, of logocentrism. And this, accordingly, was a protest against the 'linguistic turn', which, under the name of structuralism, was already well on its way . . . Deconstruction was inscribed in the 'linguistic turn', when it was in fact a protest against linguistics!
>
> (TS 76)

In truth, Derrida has always been preoccupied (in the strongest senses of that word) by what precedes or exceeds language. Sometimes he calls it 'force', as in the early essay 'Force and Signification' (1963) where he writes: 'Force is the other of language without which language would not be what it is' (FS 27). This interest in 'the other of language' is characteristic of all his work. As he summarizes it in an interview in 1981: 'deconstruction is always deeply concerned with the "other" of language. . . . The critique of logocentrism is above all else the search for the "other" and the "other of language"' (DO 123).

It is in this context that we should understand his concern with trying to think in terms of the mark rather than language. In the 1994 interview with Ferraris he says:

> I take great interest in questions of language and rhetoric, and I think they deserve enormous consideration; but there is a point at which the authority of final jurisdiction is neither rhetorical nor linguistic, nor even discursive. The notion of trace or text is introduced to mark the limits of the linguistic turn. This is . . . why I prefer to speak of 'mark' rather than of language. In the first place the mark is not anthropological; it is prelinguistic; it is the possibility of

language, and it is everywhere there is relation to another thing or relation to an other. For such relations, the mark has no need of language.

(TS 76)

Derrida's reference to 'the authority of final jurisdiction' as being in some way beyond or before language is linked to what he elsewhere talks about as the 'non-knowledge' of the moment of decision, a sense of being 'before the law' (which is something to which we shall return in Chapter 8 – though in order to see, I hope, that we have never left it).

At the same time, his emphasis on the notion of the mark raises the issue of animals and animality. Derrida's concern is to question and rethink 'the classical opposition between nature and law, or between animals alleged not to have language and man, author of speech acts and capable of entering into a relation to the law' (ATED 134). The logic of the mark goes 'beyond all human speech acts' (ATED 134). There is nothing essentially human about the mark. A mark need not be 'linguistic' in the conventional sense of that word: it might be, for example, the urine secreted by a mole in its tunnel. As Derrida puts it:

There is no society without writing (without genealogical mark, accounting, archivalization), not even any so-called animal society without territorial mark. To be convinced of this, one need merely give up privileging a certain model of writing [i.e. in the common, alphabetic, Western sense].

('ANU' 84)

At stake here is, among other things, what Derrida has referred to as 'a rather profound transformation of the concept of the "political"': it entails 'a certain type of non-"natural" relationship to others' which requires us to think, in short, that 'man is not the only political animal' (ATED 136).

OVERRUN

It is not that Derrida does not use the word 'text' (or 'writing') in its 'normal' sense, only that this sense is supplemented and displaced, from the beginning. We might see this in terms of some remarks he makes about the nature of translation and the idea of an 'original text' in the work of Walter Benjamin. Derrida comments:

> A text is original insofar as it is a thing, not to be confused with an organic or
> a physical body, but a thing, let us say, of the mind, meant to survive the death
> of the author or the signatory, and to be above or beyond the physical corpus
> of the text, and so on. The structure of the original text is survival.
>
> (EO 121)

'Text' comprises an effect of traces and remnants, marked by a ghostly logic of death and survival (or 'living on'). Derrida's attention here to a thinking of text as something other than 'an organic or a physical body' is particularly illuminating, too, for understanding what he has to say elsewhere about poetry and the poematic. (See Chapter 11.)

Derrida's notion of 'text', then, involves a displacement and over-running of any allegedly proper or conventional sense of the term. The displacement already announced in that outrageous six-word sentence in *Of Grammatology* in 1967 continues. 'The question of the text', he suggests in 'Living On' (1979), 'has been elaborated and transformed in the last dozen or so years' (LO 83). 'Living On' is one of Derrida's most delirious, breathless, overflowing essays, focused on some of the most delirious writings of Percy Bysshe Shelley (1792–1822) and Maurice Blanchot (1907–2003). (This essay appears with 'Border Lines', a similarly delirious, if more 'telegrammatic' piece running at the bottom of each page, bordering and borderlining, flowing under and over 'Living On': see LO/BL.) It is in 'Living On' that we encounter one of his most lyrical and apocalyptic declarations on the notion of text:

> a 'text' is henceforth no longer a finished corpus of writing, some content
> enclosed in a book or its margins, but a differential network, a fabric of traces
> referring endlessly to something other than itself, to other differential traces.
> Thus the text overruns all the limits assigned to it so far (not submerging or
> drowning them in an undifferentiated homogeneity, but rather making them
> more complex, dividing and multiplying strokes and lines) – all the limits, every-
> thing that was to be set up in opposition to writing (speech, life, the world, the
> real, history, and what not, every field of reference – to body or mind, conscious
> or unconscious, politics, economics, and so forth).
>
> (LO 84)

The first bit of this excerpt emphasizes that there is nothing 'bookish' about the notion of 'text' for Derrida. 'Text' is figured rather as what Geoffrey Bennington has defined as 'any system of marks, traces, referrals' (Bennington 2000, 217). The second sentence dashes away, overrunning syntactical limits, stressing that it is not a question of 'writing' as *opposed* to something else ('speech, life, the world, the real, history, and what not'), but rather of the ways in which 'speech, life, the world, the real, history, and what not' are themselves caught up in a generalized notion of writing.

At issue here is a 'concept of text' which 'no longer opposes writing to erasure' (ATED 137). This 'new' concept entails what we noted earlier as an 'unbounded generalization' (TTP 40), an extension of the 'accredited concept, the dominant notion' (LO 83) of 'text' and 'writing'. This precisely does *not* mean that we can then conclude 'everything is just writing', 'reality is merely a text', and so on. On the contrary, things become *more* not less complex. The complexity arises from having to think in new and different ways about 'limits', about margins, frames, boundaries and borderlines. We need to 're-think [the] effects of reference' (Dec 19), Derrida argues. This is not to suggest that 'there is no referent', but rather that 'the referent is textual' (Dec 19). Any thinking of the referent is inextricably caught up in the logic of that 'differential network' and 'fabric of traces' he evokes in 'Living On'. We have to reckon with the idea that 'the text is not a presence' (ATED 137). A text always remains in crucial ways 'imperceptible' (PP 63). Derrida seeks, as he puts it, to 'recast the concept of text by generalizing it almost without limit, in any case without present or perceptible limit, without any limit that *is*' (BBOL 167).

THERE IS NOTHING OUTSIDE CONTEXT

'There is nothing outside the text': as Derrida has noted, this phrase has 'for some become a slogan, in general so badly misunderstood, of deconstruction' (ATED 136). He has suggested an alternative formulation that may be less liable to misconstrual or confusion: 'there is nothing outside context' (ATED 136). Or, even more innocuous-looking perhaps: 'there is nothing but context' (Bio 873). 'Context' here can be 'speech, life, the world, the real, history, and what not': in which case, to quote Derrida, 'deconstruction would be the effort to take this limitless context into account, to pay the sharpest and broadest attention possible to context, and thus to an incessant movement of recontextualization' (ATED 136). Again here, we have the double gesture of the 'sharpest' *and* 'broadest' attention, an affirmation of the significance of minuscule

detail *and* of interminable overrun. 'No meaning can be determined out
of context, but no context permits saturation': this is what Derrida's
texts keep affirming, while always affirming it differently.

What is this structure that accounts for the fact that 'No meaning
can be determined out of context, but no context permits saturation'?
Sometimes he calls it 'text', sometimes 'writing', sometimes 'trace',
'supplement', 'differance', 'the remnant', 'iterability', 'the mark'. The
point about this chain of 'non-synonymous substitutions' (Diff 12), however, is that what we call this structure is in a crucial sense *secondary*. As
he says in 'Living On': 'I have given this structure many . . . names, and
what matters here is the secondary aspect of nomination. Nomination is
important, but it is constantly caught up in a process that it does not
control' (LO 81).

As always in Derrida's work, it is a matter of the strange, ghostly
force of what makes a mark (or text, or writing, etc.) possible. He
describes this very well in 'Limited Inc a b c . . .':

> If one admits that writing (and the mark in general) *must be able* to function in
> the absence of the sender, the receiver, the context of production, etc., that
> implies that this power, this *being able*, this *possibility* is *always* inscribed, hence
> *necessarily* inscribed *as possibility* in the functioning or the functional structure
> of the mark. . . . [T]his possibility is a *necessary* part of its structure.
>
> (LI 48)

Everything will doubtless disappear in the long run. Some marks are
more enduring than others. Indeed one of the ways in which Derrida
has suggested we might think about the enduring qualities of canonical
texts or 'great works' (in literature or philosophy or music or film or
whatever), about their capacity to 'resist erosion', is by analogy with
nuclear waste: thus he speaks of the '[e]nigmatic kinship between . . .
nuclear waste and the "masterpiece"' (Bio 845). The email message I
sent to a friend earlier today is undoubtedly less liable to last than the
writings of Thomas Hardy, but they are governed by the same structure. For, in order to function, the mark must be *marked in advance* by
the necessary possibility of the absence of the sender. Derrida calls this
'prior' inscription or marking of the mark the '*re*-mark'. This ghostly
'remark', he says, 'constitutes *part* of the mark itself' (LI 50).

ITERABILITY

At issue here is a 'structure of repeatability' or what Derrida calls 'iterability' (48). It must be possible for a mark to be repeated and still be readable, even if the author of the mark is dead. The structure of the mark consists in the fact that it is 'iterable' (47). In 'Signature Event Context' (1971) Derrida suggests that 'iterability', a word drawing together the Latin *iter* ('again') and the Sanskrit *itara* ('other'), is 'the logic that ties repetition to alterity' (SEC 7). It is always possible that I will die before my friend gets round to reading my email message, for example, but my message would still be readable. What Derrida is saying here does not apply only to what is called 'writing' or 'text' in the traditional, apparently commonsensical senses of those terms. It applies also to speech. It is what he has elsewhere referred to as 'writing in the voice' (see Dia 140). We might here consider the singular and terrible example of when someone on one of the planes that crashed into the World Trade Center on September 11 2001 left a message on their lover's voice-mail. Telephones and voice-recording technology only make more explicit, more graphic (if I may be permitted to use that word) what was always already at work in the structure of signification. 'Death' can be one name for this necessary possibility (see SEC 8). Nomination is secondary. It can also be called 'trace' or 'non-present remainder [*restance*]' (10). It is spectral: what is 'necessarily possible' is neither present nor absent, it haunts. Derrida declares:

> For a writing to be a writing it must continue to 'act' and to be readable even when what is called the author of the writing no longer answers for what he has written, for what he seems to have signed, be it because of temporary absence, because he is dead or, more generally, because he has not employed his absolutely actual and present intention or attention, the plenitude of his desire to say what he means, in order to sustain what seems to be written 'in his name'.
>
> (SEC 8)

There is what might appear an uncanny twist or torsion in this conception of writing, namely that the 'plenitude' that Derrida is talking about, the desire for 'absolutely actual and present intention or attention', the plenitude of pure presence, would be death. Our desires are oriented towards certain goals (When does this guy get to the point? When can I go home? When can we get to the bar and have a drink?).

We are, if you will, drenched in the teleological (we may recall here that *telos* is ancient Greek for 'goal', 'aim' or 'purpose'). We are impelled by desires that carry an ineffaceable *telos* brandmark. This gives rise to a double bind succinctly formulated by Derrida as follows: 'Plenitude is the end (the goal), but were it attained, it would be the end (death)' (ATED 129).

This is also where a link should be pointed out between the human and the machine: 'To write is to produce a mark that will constitute a sort of machine which is productive in turn, and which my future disappearance will not, in principle, hinder in its functioning' (SEC 8). There is a machine-like repetition or repeatability that is nevertheless marked by singularity: the context is forever altering even if in some sense the text remains the same. For something to be readable (the little piece of graffiti, for example, 'BE FREE', or the phrase 'I have forgotten my umbrella'), it must be 'structurally liberated from any living meaning' (Sp 131). In a word, it must be iterable, Derrida argues. That is to say, it must carry with it a capacity to be repeated in principle again and again in all sorts of contexts ('no context permits saturation'), at the same time as being in some way singular every time ('no meaning can be determined out of context'). Iterability thus entails both 'repetition' (sameness) and 'alterity' (difference).

SUMMARIZING IN A WINK

I began this chapter by stressing that Derrida is not a linguistic philosopher or a textualist critic, even if he is deeply interested in questions of language, linguistics, rhetoric, text, speech act theory, and so on. His celebrated, even notorious claim that 'there is nothing outside the text' needs to be understood in terms of a more general notion of text, that is to say a thinking of 'text' as 'unbounded generalization' (TTP 40). A text is a 'fabric of traces' governed by a logic of the 'nonpresent remainder', by what thus figures the impossibility of pure presence, the impossibility of absolute plenitude of meaning or intention. It is in many ways perhaps helpful to think of Derrida's work in terms of the *mark*, rather than of 'text' or 'writing' in the traditional, narrow senses of these words. The mark may be a wink, as when (this is one of Derrida's examples), 'I wink at someone while listening to my favourite music' (LI 50). The logic of the nonpresent remainder constitutes a law, Derrida suggests, that affects not only 'writing' but speech, body-language and indeed experience in general. He observes: 'I shall even extend this law to all "experience" in general if it is conceded that there is no experience consisting of *pure* presence but only of chains of differential marks' (SEC 10).

7

DIFFERANCE

In my best English I pronounce this word: 'differance'. I say 'difference with an "a"'. Derrida stresses that (in French) the difference between 'difference' and 'differance' 'cannot be heard' (Diff 3). In English too, I propose that we try to pronounce and hear it as a homophone for 'difference'. (In French it has an 'e'-acute, _différance_: I have chosen to translate it into an apparently more 'English' version.) As so often in Derrida's work, it is a question of something nevertheless going on in the voice as much as in the spectral space of page or computer-screen. Differance would be another name in the open-ended chain of 'non-synonymous substitutions' (Diff 12) that I have referred to earlier. Derrida makes the word up. And already I have misled you by referring to it as a name and as a word. His most focused and exten-sive account is in the essay of 1968 entitled 'Differance'. This essay is a sort of distillation and exposition of arguments that can be traced through _Of Grammatology_ (1967) (OG), _Speech and Phenomena_ (1967) (SP) and other earlier essays. Differance, declares Derrida in the 1968 essay, 'is neither a word nor a concept' (Diff 7). Differance, he says, 'is not a name' (26). It is misleading to pose the question of differance in terms of what _is_. Differance 'is' what makes presence possible while at the same time making it differ from itself. If this sounds a bit mind-boggling at the moment, I hereby promise to do my utmost to make it clearer as I go on. I should add, however, that differance is

– or rather, 'is' – mind-boggling, whichever way we try to come or go at it.

Here, in a couple of emancipatory, perhaps terrifying sentences, is a description of differance:

> Differance is what makes the movement of signification possible only if each so-called 'present' element, each element appearing on the scene of presence, is related to something other than itself, thereby keeping within itself the mark of a past element, and already letting itself be vitiated by the mark of its relation to a future element, this trace being related no less to what is called the future than to what is called the past, and constituting what is called the present by means of this very relation to what it is not, to what it absolutely is not: that is, not even to a past or a future as a modified present. An interval must separate the present from what it is not, in order for the present to be itself, but this interval that constitutes it as present must, by the same token, divide the present in and of itself, thereby also dividing, along with the present, everything that is thought on the basis of the present, that is, in our metaphysical language, every being, and in particular the substance or subject.

(Diff 13; cf. SP 142–3)

In what follows I hope to elucidate this formidably difficult passage by way of considering a couple of examples, concerned with the so-called everyday matter of writing (or reading) a shopping list. As always with Derrida (or with anyone else), the example is crucial. As he has remarked: 'An example always carries beyond itself: it thereby opens up a testamentary dimension. The example is first of all for others, and beyond the self' (SM 34). With my examples (which would thus not be mine), I hope to offer some sort of expository account of differance. I perhaps should stress at this preliminary point, however, that it is not a question of saying 'Look, here, some differance! Can you spot it?' Differance is the condition of the example. Indeed, it is the condition of language and meaning, the 'becoming-space of time or the becoming-time of space' (Diff 13).

ON WANTING TO BE AN INTERNATIONAL TABLE-TENNIS JUDGE

There is a perhaps deceptively straightforward moment near the beginning of an essay entitled 'Endings, Continued' (1989) – a retrospective essay on his brilliant book *The Sense of an Ending* (1967) – in which the contemporary critic Frank Kermode speaks of the 'astonishing intellectual feat' of Derrida's *Of Grammatology*. Writing as a self-conscious member of the academic 'profession', Kermode considers that Derrida's 'virtuosity is such that one sometimes feels genuinely embarrassed at claiming membership not only of the same profession but even of the same species'. He goes on to say that 'a continual attention to the operations of difference . . . may not be humanly supportable' and suggests that 'even if this is the way things really are, most of us may still have to behave as if they were otherwise' (Kermode 72–3).

Kermode touches upon something very important here, which has to do with the psychoanalytic notion of disavowal. Roughly, this can be translated as: 'I know that what Derrida is describing is true, but I am going to carry on trying to live my life as if it is not.' (This might be a fitting moment at which to stress, if only parenthetically, the crucial importance of psychoanalysis, and especially the writings of Freud, to an understanding of Derrida's work. Derrida has consistently sought to acknowledge and elaborate on the powerful and disturbing significance of psychoanalysis – whether in the context of disavowal or more generally in relation to writing and memory, psychoanalysis as an institution, the unconscious, deferred sense or effect, confession and autobiography, reason, truth and lying, desire, resistance, literature, chance and superstition, telepathy and the uncanny. See, in particular, FSW, T, SF, FV, F, MPI, GARW, MC, AF, RP, PS.) At the same time, however, these 'operations of differance' that Derrida describes are perhaps not as intimidatingly difficult to reckon with as Kermode makes out. No doubt an 'astonishing intellectual feat' makes certain demands on its reader; and no one is pretending that *Of Grammatology* – or indeed any of Derrida's other works – is a piece of cake. At any event, if Derrida is a piece of cake – and I would not wish to press the richness of this analogy too far – we should bear in mind what Friedrich Engels (1820–95) said of Hegel: 'The fellow demands time to be digested' (see Pos 76). Whether in philosophy or literature or elsewhere, the appearance of great works invariably provokes some degree of incomprehension, bafflement, mind-bogglement. Great works transform the context of their reception and this takes time. In some respects it can be said that we are still digesting Plato, unable to be sure, for example, whether or to what degree his 'pharmakon' is poison or remedy, poison *and* remedy (see PP 70ff). Plato, as Derrida has remarked, is still 'to be read, and read constantly. Plato's signature is not yet finished' (EO 87).

Kermode's notion of 'a continual attention to the operations of differance' is perhaps a little bizarre, as if one could expect of people a 'continual attention' to, for example, the unconscious or to the theory of relativity or indeed to anything or anyone in particular at all. In the days before Monty Python, there used to be a TV comedy series, involving Eric Idle, called *Do Not Adjust Your Set*. There is a certain sketch in which Idle, sporting (if I recall correctly) an Australian accent, plays the part of an international table-tennis judge. In front of the camera, but looking incessantly from left to right to left to right, he remarks with some authority and pride: 'I've been a table-tennis judge for fifteen years!' Who would want to be such a judge? How could anyone be? What is potentially misleading about Kermode's phrasing is its *presentist* character: he figures differance in terms of presence, that is to say in terms of a 'continual' – apparently undivided – 'attention' and in terms of how 'things really are'. Differance 'is' the difference of the present from itself. It is what makes the present possible *and* at the same time impossible. 'At the same time': this 'same' of 'the same time' is ghostly. The Eric Idle sketch might appear to epitomize presence, the 'continual attention' that is required of an international table-tennis judge. But this sketch, this TV recording is already ghostly. (All TV is ghostly: see *Echographies of Television* [ET].) The movement of Idle's head, and indeed his words ('I've been a table-tennis judge for fifteen years'), signify only on condition of a strange repeatability and otherness. Every turn of the head, every word, is only what it is, identical to itself and unique, insofar as it is repeatable, i.e. insofar as it is not absolutely identical to itself or unique. Think of the wink (as discussed at the end of the previous chapter). As Derrida puts it: 'What is is not what it is, identical and identical to itself, unique, unless it *adds to itself* the possibility of being *repeated* as such' (PP 168).

BLOCKING EVERY RELATIONSHIP TO THEOLOGY

Differance brings together the two notions of differing and deferring. In the beginning there will have been differance. As Derrida writes in the final chapter of *Speech and Phenomena*:

> Differance is to be conceived prior to the separation between deferring as delay and differing as the active work of difference. Of course *this is inconceivable if*

one begins on the basis of consciousness, that is, presence, or on the basis of its
simple contrary, absence or nonconsciousness.

(SP 88, my emphasis)

Like the supplement, differance is maddening. Indeed, the link between differance and the supplement is explicit in this section of *Speech and Phenomena*: 'what is supplementary is in reality differance', says Derrida: it is 'the operation of differing which at one and the same time both fissures and retards presence' (SP 88). Or as he notes also in the course of the reading of Rousseau in ' ". . . That Dangerous Supplement . . ."', 'supplement' is 'another name for differance' (OG 150). As with the supplement, then, it is a question of something that is 'neither a presence nor an absence. No ontology can think its operation' (OG 314). Differance, then, is not something to which one could devote one's 'continual attention': it is precisely 'inconceivable if one begins on the basis of consciousness'. But it should be added that Frank Kermode also has a point, concerning the extraordinary tenacity of focus and vision that characterizes Derrida's writing. Derrida's texts do indeed convey a sense of astonishing vigilance, whether it be likened to that of an insanely dedicated table-tennis judge or (perhaps less frivolously) of a 'trapeze-artist' (as he refers to himself on at least one occasion: see T 499).

'Inconceivable if one begins on the basis of consciousness? Doesn't all this sound rather religious?', you may be muttering to yourself. Certainly it appears to have been helpful to some readers of Derrida's work to understand differance as another name for God. But it would be misleading to say that differance is a name at all, insofar as 'name' implies some 'relatively unitary and atomic structure' (Diff 26). 'Differance' designates the fact that 'there is no atom' (to recall an aphoristic proposition I cited earlier: Dia 137). 'Differance', as Derrida has said elsewhere, 'is not the name of an *object*, not the name of some "being" that could be present. And for that reason it is not a concept either . . . [that is to say] the concept of some*thing*' (in Glendinning 2001, 85). If it is unnameable, it 'is not an ineffable Being which no name could approach: God, for example'. Rather, differance 'is the play which makes possible nominal effects' (Diff 26). 'It blocks every relationship to theology' (Pos 40), as Derrida remarks in an interview in 1971. Differance is to be construed as what 'puts into question the name of the name', as what derails the possibility of a 'unique name', even as it remains 'enmeshed' as a 'nominal effect', within 'the chains of substitutions of names' (Diff 26–7). It is Derrida's humble contention that 'there is no subject who is agent, author, and master of differance . . . Subjectivity, like objectivity, is an effect of differance' (Pos 28).

The essay 'Differance' is a densely allusive text. It engages with the work of Hegel, Saussure, Husserl, Emmanuel Levinas (1925–95), Alexandre Koyré (1882–1964), Gilles Deleuze (1925–95) and Jacques Lacan (1901–81), but it is based perhaps above all on the three modern critical thinkers arguably most crucial for an understanding of Derrida's work in general, namely Nietzsche, Freud and Heidegger. Derrida offers sharp and careful readings of Nietzsche, Freud and Heidegger, in order to suggest that the neologism of his title (differance) 'appears almost by name in their texts' (Diff 17). In each case it is a matter of how these thinkers 'put consciousness into question in its assured certainty of itself'. Together the writings of Nietzsche, Freud and Heidegger effect a trembling of '[the] form or epoch of presence' insofar as this is conceived as 'consciousness as meaning [*vouloir-dire*] in self-presence' (Diff 16). (We might here recall our earlier discussion of the decentring of the *ego cogito* and narcissism, in Chapter 2, and of deconstruction as earthquake, in Chapter 3.) For more than one reason, then, 'differance' ought to be in quotes. Differance is perhaps not a word, not really, not properly, not quite: it is not Derrida's, but it is not Nietzsche's, or Freud's, or Heidegger's either. We might recall here the slightly dizzying characterization of deconstruction as '[putting] into practice a vigilant but . . . general *use* of quotation marks' (SST 77). Like the nonpresent remainder or the supplement, differance is the 'concept' of what makes concepts possible. No 'key ideas' without differance.

ON MAKING A SHOPPING LIST

Let us try to elucidate this in terms of the example of the shopping list. Differance is what will have gone on in the compiling of a shopping list: it is the splitting, the differing and deferring of presence and identity. Derrida writes:

> *At the very moment* 'I' make a shopping list, I know (I use 'knowing' here as a convenient term to designate the relations that I necessarily entertain with the object being constructed) that it will only be a list if it implies my absence, if it

already detaches itself from me in order to function beyond my 'present' act and if it is utilizable at another time, in the absence of my-being-present-now, even if this absence is the simple 'absence of memory' that the list is meant to make up for, shortly, in a moment, but one which is already the following moment, the absence of the now of writing, of the writer maintaining [*du maintenant-écrivant*], grasping with one hand his ballpoint pen. Yet no matter how fine this point may be, it is like the *stigmē* [ancient Greek for 'point'] of every mark, already split. The sender of the shopping list is not the same as the receiver, even if they bear the same name and are endowed with the identity of a single ego.

(LI 49)

Walking into the supermarket, you don't have to be shopping on behalf of a friend or neighbour in order to be different from yourself. Pausing uncertainly in the aisle of frozen vegetables, looking at your list, you (the receiver) are not the same as the sender. And you knew this from the start, otherwise you would not have thought to write the shopping list. But still, you'd like to believe that the business of writing the list was really only something to jog your memory, in other words a supplement. A supplement? Supplement? What is a supplement? You have probably forgotten already: you'll have to return to an earlier aisle or chapter.

'Indeed,' Derrida goes on to say, 'were this self-identity or self-presence as certain as all that, the very idea of a shopping list would be rather superfluous or at least the product of a curious compulsion. Why would I bother about a shopping list if the presence of sender to receiver were so certain?' (LI 49). We might here draw on an ironic remark made by Edgar Allan Poe (1809–49): 'if you wish to forget anything on the spot, make a note that this thing is to be remembered' (Poe 1978a, 1114). Poe may appear to be saying the opposite of Derrida, but in both cases in fact it is a question of the strange but intimate links between writing and memory or forgetting. It is a question of writing as *pharmakon*, both 'poison' and 'remedy'. The pharmakon of writing (explored by Derrida in his extraordinary reading of Plato, in PP) is undecidably good *and* bad for the memory. Writing helps *and* hinders memory. As Derrida puts it in an interview: 'the bad *pharmakon* can always parasitize the good *pharmakon*' (RD 234). No wonder Poe had to make a note of his idea! 'Pharmakon', as we may or may not recall, also means 'recipe' (see PP 71): the shopping list is a pharmakon of sorts.

A NEW PROBLEMATIC OF CONSCIOUSNESS

'There is no present text in general', says Derrida in his great early essay 'Freud and the Scene of Writing' (1966): 'there is not even a past present text, a text which is past as having been present. The text is not conceivable in an originary or modified form of presence' (FSW 211). In order to be what it 'is', a text is an essentially vitiated, impure, open, haunted thing, consisting of traces and traces of traces: no text is purely present, nor was there some purely present text in the past (not even the shopping list serenely composed back in the peace and quiet of your home, before you went out into the hubbub of the street). As noted in the previous chapter, the structure of signification entails a logic of repeatability or iterability. Each element in the shopping list must be repeatable (otherwise you would not be able to read it): this repeatable or iterable aspect of sense-making means that the shopping list always refers to past texts and past elements (starting perhaps with the notion of a genre known as 'the shopping list'), but also to the future. But neither 'past' nor 'future' is here, or anywhere, ever, fully present. Without wanting to appear morbid, let me just recall the necessary possibility of death in this context. It is always possible that I will die in a road accident on my way to the supermarket, but my shopping list should still be readable by, for example, you (should you happen, for some sad reason, to be interested in the posthumous perusal of my shopping list). But if it is readable for you, this readability is structured in turn by *your* possible death. To recall Derrida's argument in 'Signature Event Context': '[a] writing that is not structurally readable – iterable – beyond the death of the addressee would not be writing' (SEC 7).

This possible death is not 'present' in the future any more than it is 'present' in the past: it is a question of spectrality at the origin, ghostliness as the structure of signification. It is not (or not 'simply') a matter of thinking about your death as a most unpleasant accident that might happen in the 20 minutes it takes to get to the supermarket. It is rather that every mark, every element in the shopping list you write is *positively* haunted: there is a 're-mark[ing] . . . in advance' (LI 50), a 'prior' hollowing out of the mark, thanks to which it is possible for the shopping list to remain readable, whether or not you manage to make it to the shop. The capacity for a shopping list to be read (again), in a different context, is due to the 'non-present remainder', the logic of repeatability or iterability that makes the shopping list readable in the first place. The shopping list has to be able to break with its original context, and this break is inscribed in the structure of signification. Derrida writes:

> To situate [this break or cutting off from its putative production or 'origin'] it is not necessary to imagine the death of the sender or of the receiver, to put the shopping list in one's pocket, or even to raise the pen above the paper in order to interrupt oneself for a moment. The break intervenes from the moment that there is a mark, at once.
>
> (LI 53)

Every element, every mark in a shopping list entails this notion of break, a relation to what it 'absolutely is not' (Diff 13).

Your shopping list never was purely present to you, in yourself. This is not to suggest that Derrida is suggesting we do away with the concept of presence. He loves the concept of presence, he is fascinated by it. In his singular fashion, Derrida inhabits the real world, just like other people. He goes to the bathroom, just like other people (even if what happens there, between him and the cat, for example, is different from what happens to anyone else in the world: see ATA). However 'sedentary' he may confess to being (see TS 42), Derrida has to catch trains and planes and turn up in the right place at roughly the right time, just like other people. None of us can get by without 'dates', 'timetables' or what he has referred to as 'all the codes that we cast like nets over time and space – in order to reduce or master differences, to arrest them, determine them' (AC 419). It is not a question of getting rid of the concept of presence, anymore than it is of getting rid of the human subject (the shopper, in this case).

Rather it is a question of the transformational possibilities of thinking presence, identity, the subject etc. anew and differently. Hence the newness evoked when Derrida wonders 'is any problem more *novel* today than that of consciousness?' and when he argues for the need to 'reelaborate a problematic of consciousness' (H 87, my emphasis). It is a question of what, in 'Limited Inc', he calls 'a rigorous and renewed analysis of the value of presence, of presence to self or to others, of difference and differance' (LI 49). Differance is 'to be conceived', let us recall, but 'this is inconceivable if one begins on the basis of consciousness, that is, presence, or on the basis of its simple contrary, absence or nonconsciousness'. If 'the text is not thinkable [*pensable* in the French text] in an originary or modified form of presence' (FSW 211), it is nevertheless to be reckoned with. But the reckoning is of a singular and strange kind: it is to engage with the incalculable. Differance calls for a kind of thinking that is 'uneasy and uncomfortable' (Diff 12), at odds with any 'calculus or mechanics of decision' (FSW 203).

As a strange 'logic' that brings together identity and difference, differing and deferring, repetition and otherness, differance is the ping-pong ball you can never follow: if 'differance is unthinkable', it is because 'the same and the entirely other . . . cannot be thought *together*' (Diff 19). Again, we might figure this sense of what is 'entirely other' in terms of the future. A shopping list promises to be readable in a future that requires the presence neither of its author nor of its intended receiver, a future to come, a future that is absolutely unforeseeable, unknowable, radically undetermined (cf. TS 20–1). Thus, as Derrida has put it in an interview: 'Differance is a thought which wishes to yield to the imminence of what is coming or about to come' (DA 534).

ELIZABETH BOWEN'S SHOPPING LIST

Let us turn to consider a literary example, a shopping list that appears in Elizabeth Bowen's great novel *The Death of the Heart* (1938):

> One cake of Vinolia for the bathroom,
> Half a dozen Relief nibs,
> One pot of salmon and shrimp paste (small size),
> One pan scrubber of crumpled metal gauze,
> One bottle of Bisurated Magnesia tablets (small size),
> One bottle of gravy browning,
> One skein of 'natural' wool (for Dickie's vests),
> One electric light bulb,
> One lettuce,
> One length of striped canvas to reseat a deck chair,
> One set of whalebones to repair corsets,
> Two pair of lambs' kidneys,
> Half a dozen small screws,
> A copy of the *Church Times*.
>
> (Bowen 1962, 154)

This is the shopping list of Mrs Heccomb, the lady of the house by the sea in Kent where Portia, the sixteen-year-old orphan at the heart of *The Death of the Heart*, is staying for a few months as a guest. Mrs Heccomb's shopping list may not make especially mouth-watering reading but still it is, I think, strangely poignant. It is like an old photograph: it evokes another time, things that no longer exist (not only the Bisurated Magnesia tablets but also that lettuce), creatures (salmon, shrimp, whales, lambs, people) no longer living. There is something in this shopping list of the peculiar temporality suggested by an earlier moment in the novel where we are introduced to Portia's new friend Lilian:

> Portia thought the world of the things Lilian could do . . . Lilian claimed to have few pleasures: she was at home as seldom as possible, and when at home was always washing her hair. She walked about with the rather fated expression you see in photographs of girls who have subsequently been murdered.
>
> (Bowen 51)

'Life will have been so short' (A 49), as Derrida says: it is 'as if I were dead already' (AI 215–6). Like Derrida after her, Bowen is a great thinker of mourning and deferred effect, of the ghostliness of the present and of 'death' as the condition of speech and writing.

The shopping list in *The Death of the Heart* is literary. 'Literary' does not simply mean 'fictional' or 'imaginary', for example in the sense that there never was a real Mrs Heccomb, nor any real lambs' kidneys, nor any real shop in which to purchase them, and so on. Rather, it is a question of what Derrida is referring to when he proposes that 'there is no literature without a *suspended* relation to meaning and reference' (TSICL 48). We cannot read about the pan scrubber or gravy browning or electric light bulb without connecting them with the 'real', but at the same time their relation to this 'real' is a *suspended* relation. More particularly, the literariness or literarity of Mrs Heccomb's shopping list is made legible on account of the narrative perspective in which it is presented. While we are given to understand that it is 'her' shopping list, it is perhaps not presented in her own words. It would appear that the sixteen-year-old orphan Portia is recounting this lady's purchases.

The shopping list is already someone else's. It is a shopping list *after the event*, a recounting of Mrs Heccomb's accounting, a kind of post mortem shopping list and a post mortem *of* the shopping list. There is the sense of a doubling, multiplying and dissemination of identities in the narrative voice. We cannot say for certain whose shopping list this is. It is Mrs Heccomb's shopping list and it is not. It is Portia's and it is not. It is the omniscient (or, more accurately perhaps, telepathic) narrator's and it is not. It is thus literary also in the sense highlighted by Derrida when he defines literature in terms of 'the altogether bare device of being-two-to-speak' (GT 153) or, in this case perhaps, 'being-two-to-write'. (I will come back to this definition and discuss it further in Chapter 10.)

The paragraph which culminates in the shopping list in Bowen's text commences with an explicit reference to Portia's point of view: 'To Portia, who had never seen a purse open so often . . . Mrs Heccomb's expenditure seemed princely'. The shopping list itself is preceded by the words: 'Everything was bought in small quantities, exactly as it was wanted day by day. Today, for instance, she made the following purchases' (Bowen 154). Would Mrs Heccomb write 'for the bath-room' or even 'for Dickie's vests' or 'A copy of the' rather than simply 'Church Times'? But conversely, are we to suppose that this shopping list has been written by Portia? In whose voice should we read or hear it? There are all sorts of other signs to suggest that this is a literary shop-ping list, from the ludic writerliness of the multiplicity of writing instruments ('Half a dozen Relief nibs') to the comic absurdity of the quotes around 'natural' ('One skein of "natural" wool') to the insistence of the 'one': 'One electric light bulb, One lettuce, One length of striped canvas to reseat a deck chair'. One will never know if this 'One' is Portia's or Mrs Heccomb's. Bowen's is a singular shopping list, even as it makes an example or offers a post mortem of this singularity. For the post mortem of singularity might be described as the impossibility of the singular: in other words, in order to be itself, every singularity must be essentially impure, repeatable or substitutable.

What Derrida has said about the singularity and irreplaceability of a witness applies also for thinking about the singularity of an act of writing or an act of reading: 'The example is not substitutable; but at the same time the same aporia always remains: this irreplaceability must be exem-plary, that is, replaceable. The irreplaceable must allow itself to be replaced on the spot' (Dem 41). If 'deconstruction is a coming-to-terms with literature' (Dec 9), this would be among other things because literary works such as The Death of the Heart provide an especially sharp-ened sense of this differantial logic. The only thing to be replaced is the irreplaceable. The present is out of joint with itself. There is something spooky about a shopping list. A shopping list is never one's own.

SHOPPING LIST TERMINABLE AND INTERMINABLE

I would like to conclude by coming back to the shopping list evoked by Derrida in 'Limited Inc'. We have no idea about the contents of this list: it remains abstract and cryptic. Faced with the ghostliness of Derrida's shopping list, we must reckon with the sense that there might be nothing to it, in it or on it (no 'contents') and/or that it might in fact be endless, an interminable shopping list. These two possibilities would not be mutually exclusive. In each case it is a matter of something productively unreadable, without decipherable meaning. It is, then, a question of differance as a 'thought' which 'means nothing' (OG 93), insofar as 'thought' is an *effect*, that is to say 'the effect of a *differance* of forces, the illusory autonomy of a discourse or a consciousness' (Pos 49). Differance calls for a different elaboration of questions of consciousness and presence. Derrida contends that it is something to be affirmed, 'without nostalgia', indeed with 'a certain laughter' (Diff 27). It is a matter of trying to reckon with differance as something like 'the essence of life', of life as 'trace' (FSW 203). The thinking of differance has 'not yet begun' (OG 93), he declares in *Of Grammatology*. There is 'no kingdom [*royaume*, also "realm" or "private world"] of differance': rather, it is 'threatening and infallibly dreaded by everything in us that desires a kingdom, the past or future presence of a kingdom' (Diff 22). As I have tried to stress, 'differance' cannot be a master-term or master-word: nomination is secondary, and the list is always open to supplementation, to further differentiation and multiplication. It is a question of that open-ended chain of 'non-synonymous substitutions' I referred to at the beginning of this chapter. Such a chain would include, for example, 'trace', 'text', 'writing', 'supplement', 'pharmakon', 'differance' and 'shopping list'. As Derrida has put it: 'by definition the list has no taxonomical closure' (Pos 40).

8

THE MOST INTERESTING
THING IN THE WORLD

In the course of this book I have been trying to emphasize that deconstruction is not a method, a tool or technique for reading texts,
especially not for reading literary texts. On the contrary, as Derrida has
put it: 'There is always already deconstruction, at work *in* works, especially in *literary* works' (M 123). It is not a question of deconstructing
Plato's *Phaedrus* or Joyce's *Ulysses* but rather of these texts being already
in deconstruction. Likewise, it is not a question of deconstructing the
law or institutions, but rather of thinking the law or institution as being
always already *in deconstruction*. As we saw earlier, the founding of the
United States of America (legally instituted through the Declaration
of Independence) is based on the effects of an 'undecidability between
. . . a performative structure and a constative structure' (DI 9). Or as
Derrida has said apropos of the university: 'the foundation of a university institution is not a university event' (Moc 30). Deconstruction is
not something brought in from the outside, like a band of 'special
forces': it is a foreign body, already inside. It is a kind of founding
excess, exorbitance or supplementarity.
    Literature has a peculiar but decisive role in all of this. We might
recall, once again, Derrida's succinct proposition that 'deconstruction
is a coming-to-terms with literature' (Dec 9). Literature, as he suggests
in the 1989 interview with Derek Attridge, is 'the most interesting thing
in the world, maybe more interesting than the world' (TSICL 47).

How, you may ask, can something be in the world but apparently not in it, be more interesting *than* it? We can perhaps already sense in Derrida's formulation something of the uncanny unsettling of inside and outside that is associated with the exorbitant, supplemental strangeness of deconstruction.

LITERATURE AND HISTORY

As we saw in Chapter 4, the modern conception of literature is linked up with that of democracy. Literature is a comparatively recent phenomenon: 'the institutional or socio-political space of literary production as such is a recent thing' (TSICL 40). As Derrida has put it:

> Literature is a modern invention, inscribed in conventions and institutions which . . . [secure] in principle its *right to say everything*. Literature thus ties its destiny to a certain non-censure, to the space of democratic freedom (freedom of the press, freedom of speech, etc.). No democracy without literature, no literature without democracy.
>
> (POO 23)

He stresses that '*literature* is a Latin word': the concept of literature is bound up with a 'history of latinity' (Dem 20–1) and thus with that movement of Anglo-American-based political and cultural globalization that Derrida calls 'globalatinization' (or in French *mondialatinization*: see FK, esp. 67, n.7).

Sharply attentive to its historical and cultural specificity, Derrida has shown a particular interest in European (mainly French) literary writing over the past century or so, from Stéphane Mallarmé onwards. Whether he is responding to the works of Mallarmé (DS, Mal), Antonin Artaud (1896–1948) (TC, US), Franz Kafka (BL), James Joyce (TWJ, UG), Paul Celan (1920–70) (Sh), or contemporary writers such as Philippe Sollers (Diss), Maurice Blanchot (LO, LG, Dem) or Hélène Cixous (SOO), Derrida's stress is on how these works are themselves preoccupied with questions of writing, literature or literarity. The interest of literature goes far beyond aesthetic or formalist concerns: his focus is on the importance of the literary work in having transformed and in continuing to transform the ways in which we think, for example not only about 'writing' in its narrow sense, but about history, politics, democracy and law, the world itself. The literary works to which he is most drawn are works that participate in a more general transformation, in that trembling and upheaval of western thinking that we might, provisionally, call deconstruction.

This transformation is historical but, it should be noted, it is also a transformation *of* the historical, insofar as historiography has always been founded on presence, on the history of the past as what was once present: these literary texts are also shown to be concerned with notions of the present that are strange or ghostly, with kinds of thinking and experience that fracture and disturb linear, calendrical conceptions of time and history. Thus, Derrida suggests, in the past century 'the experience of literature' has participated in a more general series of intellectual and philosophical earthquakes, 'shaking the authority and pertinence of the question "What is . . .?"' (TSICL 48). For Derrida these two questions go hand in hand, and have been especially audible since the end of the nineteenth century: not only 'What is literature?' but also 'What is the present, what is presence, what is this "is"?' Of course this questioning can be traced further back down the calendrical tunnel, even as it entails a constant wariness as regards the construction of such a tunnel. What we call Romanticism has a decisive role in the history of this questioning. Thus Rousseau's importance, for Derrida, is that he 'starts from a new model of presence: the subject's self-presence within *consciousness* or *feeling*' (OG 98). In the context of English Romanticism we might think of Samuel Taylor Coleridge (1772–1834): in this respect, it is striking that he should have described his 1797 poem *Kubla Khan* primarily as 'a psychological curiosity' rather than a work with specifically '*poetic* merits' (see Wu 1998, 522). (I discuss *Kubla Khan* in more detail later on, in Chapters 10 and 11.)

This 'new model of presence' that Derrida outlines in *Of Grammatology* is as relevant and illuminating for thinking about literature as about philosophy. In particular from Mallarmé onwards, the intractable peculiarity of 'literarity' becomes an explicit focus of works of literature. Derrida speaks, for example, of what is characteristic of the literary works of Jean-Jacques Rousseau (1712–78), Gustave Flaubert (1821–80), Stéphane Mallarmé (1842–98), Georges Bataille (1897–1962) and Maurice Blanchot, but one might equally think of a series that would move across the works of S.T. Coleridge, Edgar Allan Poe (1809–49), Charles Dickens (1812–70), Wallace Stevens (1879–1955) and the contemporary writers J.M. Coetzee and Toni Morrison. In Derrida's view, what such works

all have in common [is] that they are inscribed in a *critical* experience of literature. They bear within themselves, or we could also say in their literary act they
put to work, a question, the same one, but each time singular and put to work
otherwise: 'What is literature?' or 'Where does literature come from?' 'What
should we do with literature?'

(TSICL 41)

This preoccupation is not confined to the authors of literary works:
Derrida considers the Russian formalists to have had a decisive role in
the early twentieth century in this respect, for they too 'explicitly
formulated the question of literarity' (Pos 70). And of course some of
these twentieth-century authors I mentioned a moment ago, such as
Bataille and Blanchot, are also important literary critics or theorists.

Most of the time, however, Derrida seems to prefer trying to read
literary works rather than trying to read literary criticism (who can
blame him?). Blanchot's amazing 'story' 'The Madness of the Day'
(1949), for example, has arguably given Derrida more to talk about than
the many literary critical essays Blanchot has published. (See, in particular, LO, LG and TTBS.) But to make this sort of claim is to maintain
a vocabulary that Derrida's work itself repeatedly calls into question:
hence his 'dream of a writing that would be neither philosophy nor literature' (TSICL 73). Blanchot is perhaps another such dreamer. The most
interesting and worthwhile kinds of literary critical texts, Derrida
suggests, are those which 'belong to literature while deforming its
limits' (TSICL 52). He is not advocating that we should 'mix everything
up and give up the distinctions between all these types of "literary" and
"critical" production' (52): rather, we should acknowledge the logic of
contamination between the two. 'Good' literature, the only worthwhile
kind, in his view, is itself necessarily 'critical'. And conversely, 'good'
literary criticism always involves a certain inhabiting of the literary or
what E.M. Forster once called, in a memorable phrase, 'voluntary
surrender to infection' (see Forster 1979, 26).

REFLEXIVITY

Derrida, then, stresses a historical trajectory in which, especially since
Mallarmé, the question of literarity becomes an explicit focus of literary
works themselves. It is not, however, simply a matter of literary texts
becoming increasingly reflexive or self-reflexive, i.e. of texts turning

back upon themselves, reflecting on themselves. You would be quite 'stupid and uninformed' (TSICL 41) to believe this. Rather, it is necessary to reflect, at once more carefully and more riskily, on the nature of the reflexive. We might start with the apparently simple, neat idea of *mise-en-abyme* (literally placing-in-abyss). *Mise-en-abyme* is an heraldic term referring, for example, to a coat of arms in which a lion holds a shield and on the shield is depicted a lion holding a shield. In a literary context, we might think of, say, a novel about a novelist writing a novel. A term that is often invoked in this context is 'metafiction': metafiction is said to be reflexive or self-conscious fiction, fiction about fiction, fiction that explicitly draws attention to the idea that it is 'just' fiction. A comparable example in poetry would be a poem about poetry or about the act of writing or reading poetry. We might want to call such poetry reflexive, metadiscursive or metapoetic.

Derrida's point here is that this 'meta-' is much more divided and paradoxical than is implied by the apparent simplicity and neatness of the heraldic metaphor. As I suggested earlier on, when talking about deconstruction as a 'radical metalinguistics' (SST 76), it is a question of working with the consequences and effects of the idea that metalanguage is at once necessary and impossible. We have to have metalanguage, and yet metalanguage is never pure: there is always fissuring, internal division and contamination. A text has in some sense to mark or re-mark itself as, for example, 'a novel', or 'short story', in order to be recognized as such. In this respect it should be noted that, in Derrida's view, literature has always had a capacity for being reflexive, that is to say for marking or 're-mark[ing]' itself as 'literature' (see LG 229). The idea of a text referring to itself, reflecting on its own language and so on, is always already at odds with itself. In 'The Law of Genre' (1979), one of his essays on Blanchot's 'The Madness of the Day', Derrida elaborates the notion of 'participation without belonging' (LG 227) as a way of describing the peculiarly elliptical or non-totalizing logic by which a text refers to itself. This is perhaps most easily illustrated in the context of what he calls the 'genre-clause' (LG 231). The gesture or 're-mark' (implicit or explicit) by which a text designates itself as a novel, or short story, and so on, at once belongs and does not belong to the text it designates. It is both part of and not part of the text. It is both inside and outside, and neither exactly one nor the other.

USHERING IN

We might reflect on some of these issues in relation to the opening of
Edgar Allan Poe's 'The Fall of the House of Usher' (1839):

> During the whole of a dull, dark, and soundless day in the autumn of the year,
> when the clouds hung oppressively low in the heavens, I had been passing
> alone, on horseback, through a singularly dreary tract of country; and at length
> found myself, as the shades of the evening drew on, within view of the melan-
> choly House of Usher. I know not how it was – but, with the first glimpse of the
> building, a sense of insufferable gloom pervaded my spirit. I say insufferable;
> for the feeling was unrelieved by any of that half-pleasurable, because poetic,
> sentiment, with which the mind usually receives even the sternest natural
> images of the desolate or terrible. I looked upon the scene before me – upon
> the mere house, and the simple landscape features of the domain – upon the
> bleak walls – upon the vacant eye-like windows – upon a few rank sedges – and
> upon a few white trunks of decayed trees – with an utter depression of soul
> which I can compare to no earthly sensation more properly than to the after-
> dream of the reveller upon opium – the bitter lapse into everyday life – the
> hideous dropping off of the veil. There was an iciness, a sinking, a sickening of
> the heart – an unredeemed dreariness of thought which no goading of the imag-
> ination could torture into aught of the sublime. What was it – I paused to think
> – what was it that so unnerved me in the contemplation of the House of Usher?
> It was a mystery all insoluble; nor could I grapple with the shadowy fancies that
> crowded upon me as I pondered. I was forced to fall back upon the unsatisfac-
> tory conclusion, that while, beyond doubt, there *are* combinations of very simple
> natural objects which have the power of thus affecting us, still the analysis of
> this power lies among considerations beyond our depth. It was possible, I
> reflected, that a mere different arrangement of the particulars of the scene, of
> the details of the picture, would be sufficient to modify, or perhaps to annihi-
> late its capacity for sorrowful impression; and, acting upon this idea, I reined
> my horse to the precipitous brink of a black and lurid tarn that lay in unruffled
> lustre by the dwelling, and gazed down – but with a shudder even more thrilling
> than before – upon the remodelled and inverted images of the gray sedge, and
> the ghastly tree-stems, and the vacant and eye-like windows.

(Poe 1978b, 397–8)

These are not strictly the opening words of Poe's text. There is
the title of course, 'The Fall of the House of Usher', but there is also

an epigraph, attributed to the French poet Pierre Jean de Béranger (1780–1857): '*Son cœur est un luth suspendu;/Sitôt qu'on le touche il résonne.*' ('His heart is a hanging [or suspended] lute: as soon as it is touched, it responds.') In a sense, everything will have been inscribed in advance in the related figures of falling (the fall of the house) and suspension (the suspended lute) that occur 'before' the text itself begins.

Correspondingly, the word 'Usher' is doubtless to be read as a proper name but as soon as one touches it, so to speak, one might hear it as having ushered in, ahead of us, the question and experience of the threshold: an usher is a doorkeeper (from the Latin *ostiārius*, doorkeeper). A couple of paragraphs later, the narrator will refer to the 'title of the estate', as bearing 'the quaint and equivocal appellation of the "House of Usher"'. As Derrida has remarked: 'A title is always a promise' (M 115). When does the fall happen? When does the fall of this 'title' happen? What is the time of the fall? Has it already happened, in the very title of the work? Is it not perhaps still going on, right now? If, as Derrida has argued, 'there is no literature without a suspended relation to meaning and reference' (TSICL 48), Poe's text, from its title, epigraph and first paragraph onwards, appears to illustrate this in a double sense. It is at once an *example of* this 'suspended relation' and *about the experience of this example*. A 'suspended relation to meaning and reference' is the subject of the text. The text disturbingly ponders, analyses, reflects on the experience of precisely such a suspended relation.

It is, to use the narrator's word in the opening paragraph, 'insufferable'. The narrator says 'insufferable', but he also says 'I say insufferable': the narrative discourse re-marks itself. The opening paragraph, ushering us in, multiplies the readings of the 'fall' of the title, from its evocation of 'the bitter *lapse* into every-day life', to the rhetorical self-disputation 'I was forced to *fall* back upon the unsatisfactory conclusion . . .', to the experience of precipitous 'considerations beyond our depth' regarding 'the particulars of the scene' or 'details of the picture' that the narrator is describing.

> I reined my horse to the precipitous brink of a black and lurid tarn that lay in unruffled lustre by the dwelling, and gazed down – but with a shudder even more thrilling than before – upon the remodelled and inverted images of the gray sedge, and the ghastly tree-stems, and the vacant and eye-like windows.

Inverting and altering the conventional topos of literature as a reflection of life, the final sentence of Poe's opening paragraph provokes a sense of what Derrida has called 'duplicity without original', the uncanny as 'the wellspring of so-called fantastic literature' (SF 270).

APORIA

What is happening, what is narrated in the multiple, divided, lapsingly lapidary opening of Poe's text is, to borrow Derrida's phrasing, 'not self-mirroring or mere *mise en abyme'*. There is no 'folding back upon itself or reproducing itself within itself in perfect self-correspondence' (BL 105). Derrida encourages us to be especially circumspect with regard to the question of the abyss. As he puts it on one occasion: 'I do not believe in it very much'; we should, he suggests, be 'wary of the confidence that it inspires fundamentally' (SF 304). In Poe's text, the 'remodelled and inverted images' produce something different, 'more thrilling than before'. What is at issue here is not some comforting notion of textual navel-gazing or of what Marian Hobson calls 'tidy embedding' (Hobson 1998, 75). We are drawn rather into a thinking of the 'suspended relation' of a reflexivity without depth or bottom ('abyss' is from the ancient Greek *abyssos*, from *a* 'without', *byssos* 'depth' or 'bottom'). The abyss in this context thus corresponds with what might appear to be the quite contrary notion of aporia. 'Aporia' is loosely a rhetorical term for 'doubt' or 'difficulty in choosing', but more precisely it means a sort of absolute blockage, a 'No Way' ('aporia' again coming from ancient Greek, *a* 'without', *poros* 'way' or 'passage'). Aporia, as Derrida has described it, is 'a non-road' (FL 947). In his terms, aporia entails 'an interminable experience' (A 16). Like the experience of the undecidable, '*the aporia can never simply be endured as such*' (A 78).

His various accounts of aporia and abyss, aporia as abyss, are not confined to the question of literature: on the contrary, they are concerned with matters of life and death, law, ethics, politics and justice. They are concerned with 'put[ting] in motion a new thinking of the possible' (AIWP 361). He contends that 'a sort of nonpassive endurance of the aporia [is] the condition of responsibility and of decision' (A 16). 'If one must endure the aporia [or the abyss], if such is the law of all decisions, of all responsibilities . . . and of all the border problems that can ever arise' (A 78), it is because the aporia (or the 'disseminal abyss' [LG 250]) can never be endured. In this way we come to the brink of

Derrida's extraordinary joint-proposition: 'The ultimate aporia is the impossibility of the aporia *as such*. The reservoir of this statement seems to me incalculable' (A 78). It will already be evident, perhaps, that what pervades all this discussion of aporia or abyss, or indeed of decision and responsibility, is the question of the frame, the border or brink. Derrida's reservoir – perhaps resembling Poe's (narrator's) 'black and lurid tarn' – is incalculable, depthless, without bottom. It corresponds with what he elsewhere describes as that which is 'secret' but which 'does not conceal itself' (POO 21). (I shall come back to the question of secrets and secrecy in Chapter 10.)

BEFORE THE LAW

Let us not be overly precipitant. Let us step aside and turn to another example, Franz Kafka's short story, 'Before the Law' (written in the winter of 1914):

> Before the Law stands a doorkeeper. To this doorkeeper there comes a countryman and prays for admittance to the Law. But the doorkeeper says that he cannot grant admittance at the moment. The man thinks it over and then asks if he will be allowed in later. 'It is possible,' says the doorkeeper, 'but not at the moment.' Since the gate stands open, as usual, and the doorkeeper steps to one side, the man stoops to peer through the gateway into the interior. Observing that, the doorkeeper laughs and says: 'If you are so drawn to it, just try to go in despite my veto. But take note: I am powerful. And I am only the least of the doorkeepers. From hall to hall there is one doorkeeper after another, each more powerful than the last. The third doorkeeper is already so terrible that even I cannot bear to look at him.' These are difficulties the countryman has not expected; the Law, he thinks, should surely be accessible at all times and to everyone, but as he now takes a closer look at the doorkeeper in his fur coat, with his big sharp nose and long, thin, black Tartar beard, he decides that it is better to wait until he gets permission to enter. The doorkeeper gives him a stool and lets him sit down at one side of the door. There he sits for days and years. He makes many attempts to be admitted, and wearies the doorkeeper by his importunity. The doorkeeper frequently has little interviews with him, asking him questions about his home and many other things, but the questions are put indifferently, as great lords put them, and always finish with the statement that he cannot be let in yet. The man, who has furnished himself with many things for his journey, sacrifices all he has, however valuable, to bribe the doorkeeper.

That official accepts everything, but always with the remark: 'I am only taking it to keep you from thinking you have omitted anything.' During these many years the man fixes his attention almost continuously on the doorkeeper. He forgets the other doorkeepers, and this first one seems to him the sole obstacle preventing access to the Law. He curses his bad luck, in his early years boldly and loudly, later, as he grows old, he only grumbles to himself. He becomes childish, and since in his years-long contemplation of the doorkeeper he has come to know even the fleas in his fur collar, he begs the fleas as well to help him and to change the doorkeeper's mind. At length his eyesight begins to fail, and he does not know whether the world is really darker or whether his eyes are only deceiving him. Yet in his darkness he is now aware of a radiance that streams inextinguishably from the gateway of the Law. Now he has not very long to live. Before he dies, all his experiences in these long years gather themselves in his head to one point, a question he has not yet asked the doorkeeper. He waves him nearer, since he can no longer raise his stiffening body. The door-keeper has to bend low towards him, for the difference in height between them has altered much to the countryman's disadvantage. 'What do you want now?' asks the doorkeeper. 'You are insatiable.' 'Everyone strives to reach the Law,' says the man, 'so how does it happen that for all these many years no one but myself has ever begged for admittance?' The doorkeeper recognizes that the man has reached his end, and to let his failing senses catch the words roars in his ear: 'No one else could ever be admitted here, since this gate was made only for you. I am now going to shut it.'

(Kafka 1992, 3–4)

In his essay on this text, an essay in turn called 'Before the Law' (B) (first given as a lecture in London in 1982), Derrida proposes that there are four 'axiomatic beliefs' that constitute the conditions of consensus according to which Kafka's story is read. These are: (1) 'our recognition that the text . . . has its own identity, singularity and unity' (B 184); (2) our belief 'that the text has an author', that is to say '[t]he existence of its signatory is not fictitious, in contrast with the characters in the story' (185); (3) our belief or presupposition that 'events are related', that there is some narrative, some account or story (*récit* in French), and that this is something that we regard as belonging 'to what we call literature' (186); and (4) that '[w]e think we know what a title is, notably the title of a work' (188). Patiently and systematically, Derrida then goes on to trouble all of these axioms or presuppositions, in particular as a way of exploring a double question: 'Who decides, who judges, and according to what criteria, that this [story or account] belongs to literature?' (187).

Derrida's own account or story of 'Before the Law' is guided by the sense that

there is no such thing as a literary essence or a specifically literary domain strictly identifiable as such; . . . this name of literature perhaps is destined to remain improper, with no criteria, or assured concept or reference, so that 'literature' has something to do with the drama of naming, the law of the name and the name of the law.

(187)

Kafka's title, 'Before the Law' (*Vor dem Gesetz*), seems to dramatize this act of naming to which Derrida refers. Like all titles of literary works, 'Before the Law' is *before* the text: the title is generally taken to be above, it is the heading below or after which the literary work 'itself' is to be discovered. Like all titles of literary works, 'Before the Law' is at the same time *before the law*. We can perhaps begin to sense the strangeness of this apparent 'repetition'. It is not a question simply of reflexivity, of the title referring to itself and leaving us to ponder and admire: how clever, the title is a self-referring or self-reflexive phrase!

Like all titles of literary works, 'Before the Law' is before the law in the sense that it has a relation to the law and laws, for example to laws of copyright. As Derrida notes: 'the title of a book allows us to classify it in a library, to attribute to it rights of authorship, as well as the trials and judgments which can follow' (189). (He is here alluding to the fact that the text of 'Before the Law' also appears as a passage in Kafka's novel, *The Trial*: see B 217–20.) Like all titles of literary works, 'Before the Law' is part of the literary work in question and not part of it at the same time. It names the text, as if it were outside that text, added on to it afterwards or, as it were, added on *before* (you can perhaps feel the strange 'return of the supplement' or 'supplement at the origin' here, once again). But at the same time 'Before the Law' is *part of* the text to which it is ostensibly external. Is a title part, or not part, of the text it entitles? It is a question of the frame, border or brink. Where is the title exactly? What is its place, properly speaking? As Derrida remarks: 'We would say that the title belongs to literature even if its belonging has neither the structure nor the status of that which it entitles, to which it remains essentially heterogeneous. That the title belongs to literature does not prevent it from having legal authority' (189). Literature and law are implicated with one another, as strange mutual accomplices: there is a certain fictionality or fictionalizing at the heart of the law. This is Derrida's argument in 'Before the Law'.

A FREUDIAN DIGRESSION

He demonstrates this perhaps most memorably in a passage of his essay that might appear to be a digression (but all of Derrida's work is concerned with the appearance or apparitional effects of digression, thus with a rethinking of the digression, of what a digression is and where it could be said to belong: as he has remarked, 'dissemination' necessarily entails a rather 'ancient' 'theory of digression': see O 27). He digresses, apparently, in order to talk about Freud talking about the origin of morality. It provides a very striking example of the logic of the supplement (the supplementarity of a digression, and a sort of fictional supplementarity, a supplementary fictionality at the heart of law). Freud is compelled to tell a story but, in the act of doing so, betrays the annulment or effective impossibility of this story. Derrida quotes Freud in *Totem and Taboo* (1913) on the subject of the sons' murder of the primeval father:

> The earliest moral precepts and restrictions in primitive society have been explained by us as reactions to a deed which gave those who performed it the concept of 'crime'. They felt remorse [but how and why, if this is *before* morality, *before* law? – J.D.] for the deed and decided that it should never be repeated and that its performance should bring no advantage. This creative sense of guilt still persists among us. We find it operating in an asocial manner in neurotics, and producing new moral precepts and persistent restrictions, as an atonement for crimes that have been committed and as a precaution against the committing of new ones . . . What lie behind the sense of guilt of neurotics are always *psychical* realities and never *factual* ones. What characterizes neurotics is that they prefer psychical to factual reality and react just as seriously to thoughts as normal people do to realities.
>
> (Freud 1985, 222; partially quoted in B 197–8)

This is Freud's account, his story of the origin of morality. Derrida explores the implicit double bind in Freud's thinking here, namely that 'the best way of keeping [the father] alive [is] to murder him'. 'Failure', as Derrida comments, is for Freud 'conducive to moral reaction' (see Freud 1985, 204, n. 1).

Describing and subtly transforming Freud's story, Derrida goes on:

> Thus morality arises from a useless crime which in fact kills nobody, which comes too soon or too late and does not put an end to any power; in fact, it inaugurates nothing since repentance and morality had to be possible *before* the crime. Freud appears to cling to the reality of an event, but this event is a sort of non-event, an event of nothing or a quasi-event which both calls for and annuls a narrative account.

(B 198)

Derrida's point here is not that Freud is being simply naïve or nostalgic in his concern to return to the origin, here in his fabrication of a story about the origin of morality. As with other readings (such as 'Freud and the Scene of Writing' [FSW], 'Speculations – on "Freud"' [SF] and *Archive Fever* [AF]), Derrida's account is impelled by a profound admiration for Freud's writing and respect for the value and importance of Freudian psychoanalysis. 'Let Us Not Forget – Psychoanalysis' (LUNFP) is the title of one of Derrida's most succinct statements on this topic.

As always, also, however, he is concerned with a deconstructive labour of love. As he puts it: 'I love very much everything that I deconstruct . . . the texts I want to read from a deconstructive point of view are texts I love' (EO 87). His reading of Freud in 'Before the Law' is one that in some sense betrays Freud by being true to him. Derrida's reading brings out a sense of Freud-beside-himself, showing that Freud's text is saying 'more, less, or something other than what he *would mean* [or would want to say: *voudrait dire*]' (OG 158). In short, it testifies to Derrida's argument (as we have explored it elsewhere in the present book) that 'blindness to the supplement is the law' (OG 149).

The passage from *Totem and Taboo* is one of those moments in Freud's writing that can leave us with a fleeting, curious or eerie feeling that it was written especially 'for' Derrida, as if waiting for him to come along and point it out. Freud is apparently blind to the figure of the supplement that he is nevertheless effectively theorizing. The sons who murdered the father 'felt remorse for the deed', says Freud, prompting Derrida's supplementary queries: 'but how and why, if this is *before* morality, *before* law?' Freud's account depends on a logic of the supplement. In tacitly proposing that 'repentance and morality had to be possible *before* the crime', Freud's text is not thereby rendering itself as simply nonsense. Rather, it demands to be understood in terms of the notion of what Derrida calls an event 'that one is compelled neither to believe nor disbelieve', an 'uncanny' deed that 'must be somehow spun from fiction' (B 198–9).

Derrida seeks to be faithful to Freud's own early insight (formulated in a letter to Wilhelm Fliess in 1897) that 'there are no indications of reality in the unconscious, so that one cannot distinguish between truth and fiction that has been cathected with affect' (quoted in B 192). In the case of Freud's story about the origin of morality, it is not primarily a question of the author's 'intentions', of ' "Did he believe in it or not? did he maintain that it came down to a real and historical murder?" and so on' (199). Instead, what Freud's account brings to light (regardless of what he himself might have thought he was saying) is the sense of an 'event without event', a 'pure event where nothing happens', an event which 'nobody would have encountered . . . in its proper place of happening'. This strange non-event that 'would instate the law, the two fundamental prohibitions of totemism, namely murder and incest' thus 'resembles a fiction' (199), a narrative that is at once demanded and annulled. Freud's 'story' is, as Richard Beardsworth has put it, 'less the narration of an imaginary event than the *simulacrum of narration*' (Beardsworth 1996, 37). 'This quasi-event', Derrida argues, 'bears the mark of fictive narrativity' – at once of fictional narrative and of narrative as fictive. As such, he suggests, 'it is the origin of literature at the same time as the origin of law' (B 199).

THE DISCIPLINE OF READING

'The law is fantastic', argues Derrida, it 'remains essentially inaccessible' (199). If blindness to the supplement is the law, it would seem that the law 'is' at the same time that before which *one can never be*. Derrida's apparent digression in relation to Freud and psychoanalysis in fact takes us to the heart of literature and to the heart of Kafka's fantastic text. Like Freud's account and like Kant's conception of moral law (to which Freud's account is explicitly indebted), Kafka's 'Before the Law' is concerned with a sort of double logic. On the one hand, 'the law as such should never give rise to any story. To be invested with its categorical authority, the law must be without history, genesis, or any possible derivation.' On the other hand, '[one] cannot be concerned with the law, or with the law of laws . . . without asking where it has its place and whence it comes' (B 191).

Kant, Freud, Kafka: what makes all of these thinkers important for Derrida has to do with how each in their different way brings out a ghostly or virtual 'narrativity and fiction' at 'the very core of legal thought' (190). This notion of 'in their different way' is also crucial. As Derrida puts it: 'The law is always an idiom, and this is the sophistication of Kant's thought. Its door concerns only you' (B 210). Or to put it in another way: every usher is a stranger only for you. Kafka's story beautifully, even frighteningly stresses that one's relation to the law is singular: 'The doorkeeper recognizes that the man has reached his end, and to let his failing senses catch the words roars in his ear: "No one else could ever be admitted here, since this gate was made only for you. I am now going to shut it."' The gate or door to the law is for this countryman and no one else. As the contemporary critical thinker Rodolphe Gasché has described it, in a fine essay on these Kafka and Derrida texts, 'singularity is the condition under which there can be something like a law at all, a law that is pure, nonrepresentable, and as such, in purity, inaccessible' (Gasché 1999, 297). The door of the law is singular, only for you; but you can never be in the presence of the law. This is the law of the law.

Let me just emphasize that all of this is not to suggest that Derrida is thus advocating anarchy or disrespect for the law. On the contrary one cannot begin to understand what his work is about without a respect for the 'norms of the discipline of reading' (TS 42). As he puts it:

Even when I give the impression of transgressing, putting into question, displacing, it is always under [the] authority [of these norms], with a sense of responsibility in the face of a certain philological morality, before a certain ethics of reading or of writing. In short: before the law.

(TS 43)

Among other things, a disciplined reading of Kafka's 'Before the Law' enables Derrida to offer an especially clear account of differance. The man from the country must wait: access to the law is deferred. This deferral constitutes what Derrida calls 'an interminable differance . . . differance till death' (B 204). He writes:

> What is delayed is not this or that experience, the access to some enjoyment or to some supreme good, the possession or penetration of something or somebody. What is deferred forever till death is entry into the law itself, which is nothing other than that which dictates the delay. . . . What *must not* and cannot be approached is the origin of differance: it must not be presented or represented and above all not penetrated. That is the law of the law. . . . It is neither natural nor institutional; one can never reach it, and it never reaches the depths of its original and proper taking-place.
>
> (205)

Such would be the abyss, the 'cryptic' (205) abyss, of differance.

LITERATURE AND THE LAW

It does not matter if you are a student of literature or a police officer, judge or prime minister, king or queen: everyone is before the law, but no one is ever in the presence of the law. 'The law is mad', as Derrida has remarked on numerous occasions (see, for example, LG 251, MO 10): Kafka's story perhaps lets us feel something of this madness. In an important essay entitled 'Force of Law: The "Mystical Foundation of Authority"' (1990), Derrida has argued that it is necessary to think deconstructively about the 'force of law', acknowledging the 'performative and therefore interpretative violence' (FL 941) in the founding or instituting of any law, acknowledging in particular what he has elsewhere called 'the impossibility for a principle of grounding to ground itself' (PR 9). Derrida notes that language is 'the elementary medium of the law' (B 206) and stresses that 'law is deconstructible' (FL 943) (unlike justice, about which I shall say more in the following chapter). In the globalatinizing so-called 'western world', it is the name of the Christian 'God' that has for so many centuries provided the final resting place, the ultimate 'authority' for making and keeping the law.

Literature has a strange but crucial place in relation to thinking about law. As I have tried to make clear, literature has no essence: what we call 'literature', as Derrida sees it, 'has something to do with the drama of naming, the law of the name and the name of the law' (B 187). In recent work such as *Demeure: Fiction and Testimony* (1998) Derrida has extended his analysis of literature and law, specifically in relation to testimony and bearing witness. He seeks to deconstruct, to disturb and transform the apparently commonsensical view that, 'in our European juridical tradition, testimony should remain unrelated to literature and especially, in literature, to what presents itself as fiction, simulation, or simulacra' (Dem 29). In particular he argues that, 'if the testimonial is by law irreducible to the fictional, there is no testimony that does not structurally imply in itself the possibility of fiction, simulacra, dissimulation, lie and perjury – that is to say, the possibility of literature, of the innocent or perverse literature that innocently plays at perverting all of these distinctions' (Dem 29). It is not simply a matter of suggesting that literature can be a mischievous or subversive discourse that plays about with the law or with the truth – with, for example, the idea of telling the truth, the whole truth and nothing but the truth. The place of literature is altogether less *placeable*. 'Literature', in the neologistic sense in which Derrida formulates it, is at once more significant and spectral. There can be no 'truthful testimony' without the *possibility* of fiction. As he puts it: 'the possibility of literary fiction haunts so-called truthful, responsible, serious, real testimony as its proper possibility. This haunting is perhaps the passion itself, the passionate place of literary writing, as the project to say everything' (Dem 72).

9

MONSTERS

PROSPECTUS

In an essay on John Keats (1795–1821), first published in 1966, Paul de Man suggests that this English poet should be regarded as a 'prospective' writer. By this he means to contrast him with poets whose work is 'retrospective', such as William Wordsworth (1770–1850). He proposes that Keats's work 'consists of hopeful preparations, anticipations of future power rather than meditative reflections on past moments of insight and harmony' (de Man 1989, 181). Keats's work, he suggests, is 'totally oriented toward the future' (183). The critical phrase most often associated with de Man's own work is 'blindness and insight', and it has been often said that this entails a deconstructive logic: every literary, critical or philosophical text is a work of blindness and insight, in which the moments of greatest authorial insight are characteristically moments of blindness, or vice versa (see de Man 1983). His characterization of Keats is thought-provoking in this respect. The notion of the prospective writer perhaps requires to be taken with a pinch of mellow fruitfulness, for the work of every writer can no doubt be construed in these terms. But as de Man's essay makes clear, it is certainly a critically illuminating thesis in the case of Keats.

De Man does not advance a general argument here, but we might pause to consider whether there are not other writers whose work seems to be of a 'prospective character' (192). De Man himself would be a striking example of a prospective writer: there are significant shifts in his thinking and language from early to later writings. Sigmund Freud would be another: his œuvre shows great consistency but also communicates the sense of someone who kept changing, modifying his views and ideas, making new discoveries. (We might think, in this context, of Freud's renunciation of hypnosis; his elaboration of the so-called 'second topography', i.e. of the notions of id, ego and super-ego; his promulgation in and after *Beyond the Pleasure Principle* [1920] of the theory of the death drive; his 'conversion' in the 1920s to belief in telepathy; and so on.) Jacques Derrida is fascinating in this context, because he seems singularly non-prospective. He presents the rather awesome case of someone having everything sewn up from the start. His work seems, from the beginning, to be all of a piece, even if it is not a piece that we could characterize as unified, finished or finishable. There is something almost incredibly consistent, always already *in place*, about Derrida's work.

In saying this, the last thing I want to suggest is that his work is somehow timeless, 'outside history'. On the contrary, as I have been trying to make clear throughout this book, what Derrida does ('deconstruction' if you like) is informed by 'the sharpest sense of history' (SST 77). His texts are almost invariably 'occasional', in the sense that they are *responses* to specific invitations to write or speak, at specific times and in specific places (see TS 65). His work is distinctly, often explicitly dated in this way. It is consistently concerned with acknowledging and elucidating its relation to history. This entails not only an engagement with the general history of Western philosophy, but also a deeply marked embeddedness within, and indebtedness to, more recent historical 'events' such as Marxism, psychoanalysis and phenomenology. And it is also clear that there *are* shifts, new developments, changes of focus and concern in Derrida's work. One that we have already noted is the impact on Derrida's work of speech act theory, a shift that Rodolphe Gasché has tentatively called his 'performative turn' (Gasché 1999, 288; cf. Weber 1987). Another would be the impression, which Derrida himself vouches for, that his work has become more 'political', that he 'pose[s] the question of the institution more and more, in terms of both theory and practice' (TS 49). Books published in the 1990s, such as *Specters of Marx* (1993) and *Politics of Friendship* (1994), and his more recent seminars on hospitality, forgiveness, lying and perjury, the death penalty, and the democracy to come, would appear to corroborate this. (For examples of some of this more recent thinking, see Hos, OCF, N and WA.) But as he also points out, 'everything that links deconstruction to the question of the apparatus of the institution is already present in *Of Grammatology*' (TS 49). Deconstruction was always already political through and through. It entails what Geoffrey Bennington calls 'an irreducible conceptual politics': deconstruction, as he puts it, 'generalizes the concept of politics so that it includes all conceptual dealings whatsoever' (Bennington 2001, 206–7).

The earthquake-effects of deconstruction have from the beginning been political, then, not only in terms of having recognizably political aims and aspirations (starting out, perhaps, as a teaching, a teaching that questions and seeks to transform institutions, to change how we think and what we do), but also in terms of transforming the concept of the political as such. Correspondingly, Derrida may not have used the vocabulary of speech act theory in his earliest writings, but all of his texts can be considered as what he calls 'performative performances' (TS 65). His work has been engaged in the business of transformation and reinvention at least since the publication of *Of Grammatology* in 1967. As Richard Beardsworth puts it, specifically in terms of the notion of writing (*écriture*), in his book *Derrida and the Political*: 'Through his emphasis on *écriture* Derrida [has] both reinvented the relations and spaces between philosophy and literature and opened up a new field of inquiry into textual processes, these processes exceeding traditional distinctions between the real and the fictional, the historical and the imaginary' (Beardsworth 1996, 2).

Some thinkers change their minds, rejecting or significantly reworking their own earlier ideas and arguments. Some develop in stylistically distinctive ways. It is difficult to see Derrida fitting comfortably into any such categories. To increase the discomfort, indeed, his work consistently questions how we define thinking, changing one's mind, rejection and reworking, earlier and later, ideas and arguments, development and style. In a disarming and peculiar way, Derrida at the same time gives the sense of someone who seems to have grasped everything in advance and never really altered his views on anything. As he remarks, for example, in a discussion in *The Ear of the Other*, in 1979: 'I never repudiate anything, through either strength or weakness, I don't know which; but, whether it's my luck or my naiveté, I don't think I have ever repudiated anything' (EO 141–2). In an interview in 1994 he recalls that '[t]he question of writing was already announced in my higher studies dissertation of 1954' and suggests that 'in everything I've published there are always touchstones announcing what I would like to write about later on – even ten or twenty years later on' (TS 46). Almost everything that one might think of as distinctive of such and such a book or essay by Derrida can be seen as a grafting or extension, supplement or prosthesis, an outgrowth from somewhere else, earlier on.

As the word 'outgrowth' might intimate, there is perhaps something faintly monstrous about this. Just as Freud, on first arriving in the US in 1909, allegedly quipped that he and colleagues were bringing the plague (aka 'psychoanalysis'), so deconstruction, as it emerges from the work of Derrida, can give the impression of a sort of interminable growth, endlessly attaching itself, infecting and contaminating all recognizable discourses, hearts and minds, institutions and practices. There is something essentially parasitical about deconstruction. As Derrida has remarked: 'deconstruction is always a discourse about the parasite' (RD 234). It can seem that there is nothing-outside-Derrida's-text, no text, no object, no subject, no idea that his work has not touched upon or tampered with. (In the double-text 'Living On/Border Lines' he recalls Mallarmé's declaration that poetry has been touched or interfered with: 'On a touché au vers' [LO 83]. Derrida links notions of tampering with language to what he calls 'the deconstruction of a pedagogical institution and all that it implies' [BL 94].) Even when he is writing about notions of the untouchable (in relation to the 'law', in 'Before the Law', or the 'original' text which presents itself as the task of the translator, in 'DTB'), Derrida alters our thinking of that untouchable. Even 'justice', which is said to be 'undeconstructible' (FL 945, TS 56), is a relentless and explicit focus of Derrida's concern, especially in more recent texts. But then, as he has also argued, 'deconstruction' has always been concerned with 'the problem of justice': from the beginning, it 'has done nothing but address [this problem]' (FL 935). I will come back to this question at the end of this chapter.

Derrida's work seeks to make legible the monstrosities of the world, of politics, philosophy, literature and so on. Monstrousness, however, is not only or not simply what is hideous or horrible. A comparison with Shakespeare may be helpful here. Like Shakespeare's, Derrida's achievement seems unnatural, prodigious, gigantic, extraordinary, abnormal. There are at least two other respects in which their writings might be felt to correspond on the subject of monsters and monstrosity. Both writers are concerned with a performative exploration of the concept of monstrosity as a monstrosity of conception. For both, also, monstrosity appears to be above all a question of the future.

If Derrida gives the impression that his work is a sort of interminable unfolding and that each of his texts communicates with every other one in an abnormally precise and 'knowing', self-echoing or self-anticipating, intratextual fashion (thus again, I would suggest, like Shakespeare's), it should also be noted that every one of his texts is distinctive, singular, obviously different from all the rest. The reason for this is not only that every text he writes is a response or attempt to countersign another text or other texts, another author or a different situation or scene of reading, but also that he is constantly starting all over again, every time he writes. There is, in other words, something extraordinarily humble, almost monstrously un-monstrous about Derrida's writing. And in this, Derrida transpires as more Keatsian than my initial sketch of the prospective writer might have suggested. In particular, to adapt the words of de Man, Derrida is like Keats in that he seems 'haunted by a dream that always remains in the future' (de Man 1989, 181).

HOW TO WRITE

Derrida has said that, with every text he writes,

> it is really as if I had never written anything before, or even known how to write. . . . Each time I begin a new text, however modest it may be, there is dismay in the face of the unknown or the inaccessible, an overwhelming feeling of clumsiness, inexperience, powerlessness.
>
> (MMW 352)

It is undoubtedly more easily said than done, but what Derrida effectively offers here is a lesson in how to write. Be scared, be really quite scared; but be free, for here is a freedom that has never come until now, until this singular, disjointed now of writing at this very moment. Everything is at stake right now. What tone will you adopt, knowing that it is perhaps more strictly the case that this tone will adopt you? Everything, Derrida suggests, begins from this question of tone (see MO 48). His feelings of dismay and inexperience are perhaps instructive. They testify to a logic that runs throughout his work, namely that of the singular and general.

On the one hand there is this general sense that Derrida is 'repeating the same thing all the time' (TS 47) and that everything has been thought through from the start. On the other hand, there is the singularity of this blank page or computer screen right now, the sense that every text one writes is 'completely new', that whenever one writes one has to 'start all over again' (TS 47). One cannot count on anything one has said before. There is, for Derrida, 'a feeling of absolute freshness', a sense of being 'an absolute beginner' (TS 70) every time. What goes for writing also goes for teaching. He has said that when he is teaching, he has the feeling that the text he is reading and discussing is one that he is now reading 'really . . . for the first time in [his] life' (TS 47). This demanding 'freshness' is linked to Derrida's argument that the very concept of the university is at stake in every class, seminar and lecture. (See, for example, Moc 22.) The value and purpose of the university remains to be invented every day. The same applies, Derrida emphasizes, to what is called the 'freedom of the press', 'freedom of speech', 'freedom of thought', democracy itself (see OH 98).

We might recall our earlier discussion (in Chapter 4) of the links between democracy and the concept of literature as 'the right to say everything', and note an integral further link here with the concept of the university. As Derrida puts it: 'the right to say everything (or not to say everything) . . . founds both democracy and the idea of unconditional sovereignty claimed by the university' (UWC 232). (For a fuller sense of Derrida's constant preoccupation with the importance of questions of the university, teaching and education, see in particular Moc, PR, UWC and WAP.)

To write, to speak, to teach: all of these involve an encounter with incalculable possibilities of the performative. In the early essay 'Force and Signification' (1963), Derrida quotes the phenomenologist Maurice Merleau-Ponty (1908–61): 'My own words take me by surprise and teach me what I think' (quoted in FS 11). He then begins a new paragraph: 'It is because writing is *inaugural*, in the fresh sense of that word, that it is dangerous and anguishing. It does not know where it is going' (FS 11). For Derrida, this is the singular situation every time: one does not know what is coming, even within the alleged punctuality of a sentence. As he has put it: 'By the end of the sentence, it's no longer the same sentence that it was at the beginning' (EO 158). Every performative is thus a deformed performative insofar as it has to be open to, or haunted by, the incalculable, the unforeseeable or 'unanticipatable'

(Ja 41). Such is the strange freedom from which Derrida sets out as a 'critical thinker', and this is where monstrosity comes in. As he declares at the beginning of *Of Grammatology*: 'The future can only be anticipated in the form of an absolute danger. It is that which breaks absolutely with constituted normality and can only be proclaimed, *presented*, as a sort of monstrosity' (OG 5). Derrida's 'feeling of absolute freshness', of being 'an absolute beginner', is no doubt linked to this sense of 'absolute danger'. You never know what sort of text he is going to come up with next. Derrida's stress on the 'dangerous and anguishing' experience of writing perhaps helps to clarify the remarkable variety of different kinds of text that he has written – quite traditional-looking, scholarly essays (as in OG, SP, SM, PF), works presented as double-texts, in split columns or sections (such as G, TP and LO/BL), collections of aphorisms (such as AC), diary and other autobiographical fragments (such as Bio and C), postcards and related epistolary texts (such as E and T), and so on.

IN FUTURE

One of the problems, perhaps the greatest problem of all, in trying to provide an introductory account of Derrida's work lies in how to deal with the inevitable but quite misleading impression that his thinking, his texts and 'ideas' can be boxed up, systematized or simply, in a word, described. As if his work could be described without being transformed or deformed, or as if his work were only contingently or subsidiarily to do with transformation or deformation. As I have tried to make clear, description and transformation are not opposites. Derrida's work is about the ceaseless destabilization of any context, the necessary possibility of the unanticipatable that is the condition of any writing or reading.

It would be misleading also to say that his work *resists* systematization. As he has commented:

> deconstruction, without being anti-systematic, is on the contrary, and never-theless, not only a search for, but itself a consequence of the fact that the system is impossible. . . . [It is] a question of showing that the system does not work, and that this dysfunction not only interrupts the system but itself accounts for the desire for system, which draws its *élan* from this very disad-joinment or disjunction.

(TS 4)

Systematicity was always already impossible. The search for the system is itself a consequence of that fact. As Derrida has more than once remarked, recalling and reinventing Shakespeare's phrase: 'the time is out of joint' (see, in particular, SM and TOJ). One way of trying to clarify this is in terms of the future. We may think, or prefer to think, that the future is relatively predictable: sooner or later this chapter is going to come to an end, in a little while we can stop thinking about deconstruction, go home and watch the telly or whatever. This, in Derrida's terms, would not be the future, but rather the unfolding of what is predicted, expected, calculated. Deconstruction, Derrida suggests, has to do with 'the opening of the future itself' (Aft 200). In this context it is perhaps worth noting his consistent stress on the links, in French, between the word *l'avenir* (the future) and what is *to come* (*venir*, the *à-venir*) (see, for example, PIO 28–9). The future is what is to come, it is unknowable. It is not something that 'allow[s] itself to be modalized or modified into the form of the present' (Aft 200). The future, for Derrida, is thus linked to a sense of what has yet to be invented (see, in particular, PIO). In political terms this entails a commitment to thinking about democracy as the 'democracy to come', a thinking of politics (of democracy, justice and rights, borders, hospitality, immigration, national and personal identity and so on) in relation to what he calls the *arrivant*.

THE ARRIVANT

In an interview with Elisabeth Weber in 1990, Derrida puts it like this:

> the future is necessarily monstrous: the figure of the future, that is, that which can only be surprising, that for which we are not prepared . . . is heralded by species of monsters. A future that would not be monstrous would not be a future; it would already be a predictable, calculable, and programmable tomorrow. All experience open to the future is prepared or prepares itself to welcome the monstrous *arrivant*.
>
> (PTP 386–7)

The word *arrivant* (literally, 'that which or the one who arrives') is a comparatively late arrival in Derrida's work: it is perhaps first discussed in detail in *Aporias* (1993). But to say that it arrives at this or that point in the chronological unfolding of Derrida's œuvre can at best only be a mild witticism. The figure of the *arrivant* haunts everything he has ever said about the future and thus everything he has ever said about anything at all.

Like the word 'arrive', 'arrivant' has to do with what comes to the shore (from the Old French *ariver* 'to reach shore', from the Latin *ad* 'to', *rīpa* 'shore'). The question of the monstrous arrivant is a question of the border or threshold, of who or what comes to the shore or turns up at the door. Derrida is concerned with trying to think the *arrivant* in an 'absolute' sense, as what 'does not yet have a name or an identity'. This 'absolute *arrivant*' is 'not an intruder, an invader, or a colonizer'. It is 'not someone or something that arrives, a subject, a person, an individual, or a living thing' (A 34). Rather the *arrivant* is 'hospitality itself' (A 33). As Derrida puts it elsewhere, it is a matter of 'absolute hospitality', of saying 'yes' or 'come' (or, perhaps, 'be free') to the *arrivant(e)*, in other words 'to the future that cannot be anticipated' (SM 168). The *arrivant* does not come to a place named or determined in advance, but rather 'affects the very experience of the threshold' (A 33). The *arrivant* 'surprises the host – who is not yet a host or an inviting power – enough to call into question . . . the very border that delineated a legitimate home' (A 34), the home-shore or the door and threshold of one's home.

Monsters lurk everywhere in Derrida's work, at and in the borders of his work: his work is precisely 'on this border' (A 35). This is where Derrida lives, this is life *chez Derrida*. And it entails a sense of 'life' in which it is never possible finally to distinguish between the figure of the *arrivant* or of the dead or of the revenant (the ghost, that which returns). Pulling the carpet from beneath what one might have thought were one's feet, as it were, Derrida's most radical insight here is that the absolute *arrivant* 'makes possible' all the things to which one might be tempted to reduce it, including 'the humanity of man', all forms of 'belonging' (cultural, social, national, sexual), the shore, the door, the concepts of 'ego, person, subject, consciousness, etc.' (A 35). There is no event, no name or identity without the singularity of the monstrous *arrivant*.

In case any of this leaves you thinking that Derrida is just interested in frightening us, or frightening himself, let me stress that his concern with notions of monstrosity or the 'monstrous *arrivant*' is intimately connected with what is normal, with normality and normalization. This is, if you will, what lends his account such 'uncanniness' (see, for example,

A 33, SM 168): it is a question of an 'economy' of the uncanny (see EO 156–7), of rethinking the supposed opposition of the normal or familiar and the monstrous or unrecognizable. As he puts it in a lecture given in 1987: 'A monstrosity can only be "mis-known" (*méconnue*), that is, unrecognized and misunderstood. It can only be recognized afterwards, when it has become normal or the norm' (SST 79).

UNACCEPTABLE, INTOLERABLE AND INCOMPREHENSIBLE

If Derrida is concerned with writing and monstrosity, if deconstruction is a kind of monstrous thinking, oriented towards a certain experience of the monstrous, towards what he evokes, at the end of the 1966 essay 'Structure, Sign and Play in the Discourse of the Human Sciences', as 'the formless, mute, infant, and terrifying form of monstrosity' (SSP 293), this is necessarily with a view towards a movement of domestication, appropriation and assimilation. Let me pick up again from the passage I was quoting a few moments ago, where Derrida is talking about the future and the monstrous *arrivant*. He says:

> All experience open to the future is prepared or prepares itself to welcome the monstrous *arrivant*, to welcome it, that is, to accord hospitality to that which is absolutely foreign or strange, but also, one must add, to try to domesticate it, that is, to make it part of the household and have it assume the habits, to make us assume new habits. This is the movement of culture. Texts and discourses that provoke at the outset reactions of rejection, that are denounced precisely as anomalies or monstrosities are often texts that, before being in turn appropriated, assimilated, acculturated, transform the nature of the field of reception, transform the nature of social and cultural experience, historical experience. All of history has shown that each time an *event* has been produced, for example in philosophy or in poetry, it took the form of the unacceptable, or even of the intolerable, of the incomprehensible, that is, of a certain monstrosity.
>
> (PTP 387)

Philosophy can be monstrous, poetry can be monstrous. Whenever such monstrosity comes about, it constitutes an 'event', though this event does not happen *in the present*: it 'can only be recognized afterwards'. Monstrosity belongs, if it can be said to belong, to a time that is out of joint.

'A monstrosity never presents itself' (SST 79), Derrida stresses, for 'as soon as one perceives a monster in a monster, one begins to domesticate it' (PTP 386). This 'time of the monster' is especially significant for him because it is clearly aligned with the law of differance, a movement of deferral and disjointedness or disjointingness that 'never presents itself'. The alignment is a matter of more than one line. As early as 1963 we find him quoting the French Romantic painter Eugène Delacroix (1798–1863) in an epigraph: 'There are lines which are monsters. . . . A line by itself has no meaning; a second one is necessary to give expression to meaning. Important law' (see FS 15). This is also why Derrida is able to suggest that 'the coming of the monster submits to the same law as [that of] the date' (PTP 386). (We might here recall my earlier discussion of the strangeness of a date, such as 'September 11': see Chapter 1.)

It is more or less a truism that Derrida's work has been identified with the 'unacceptable', 'intolerable' and 'incomprehensible'. (This is perhaps especially the case with people who do not actually *read* his texts.) It is also evident that Derrida is passionately interested in what, in philosophy, poetry and elsewhere, is considered 'unacceptable', 'intolerable' and 'incomprehensible', in other words in some sense monstrous. For Derrida, this monstrousness has to do with what is not presentable (in the strongest sense of that phrase), with the very coming of the future, with words not written, the blank page or screen. This is not to suggest that all Derrida is really interested in doing is 'writing monstrous texts' (PTP 386), any more than one would think of Shakespeare in this way. But like Derrida, Shakespeare is a great thinker of monsters.

What might first spring to mind in this context would be characters such as Iago, Edmund and Macbeth, those 'monstrous malevolences' that the contemporary literary critic Harold Bloom has called 'artists of the self' (Bloom 1994, 64). Shakespeare is relentlessly concerned with making up monsters, with what is 'unacceptable', 'intolerable' and 'incomprehensible' in characters, art and self. He also demonstrates a profound sense of the monstrous in relation to the future. In *King Lear*, Albany tries to articulate his sense of how Gonoril and Regan have behaved:

If that the heavens do not their visible spirits
Send quickly down to tame these vile offences,

It will come,
Humanity must perforce prey upon itself,
Like monsters of the deep.

(Scene 16, 45–9)

This apocalyptic, monstrous image is of the future, of what, perhaps, 'will come'. If we feel that *King Lear* conveys a singular and unprecedented sense of the 'unacceptable', 'intolerable' or 'incomprehensible', this is not so much a *fait accompli*, but rather an experience awaiting each new reading or viewing of the play. Shakespeare's plays are what might be called (to borrow a phrase from Derrida) 'machines for repeating' (Dia 145); but each repetition is singular and different, a 'start[ing] all over again' (TS 47), a new encounter or encounters with the 'opening of the future itself'.

There are monsters in the works, in the wings, in the offing. When Iago says, at the end of the first Act of *Othello*, 'It is ingendered. Hell and night/Must bring this monstrous birth to the world's light' (1.3.385–6), he is talking about what is to come. Like a diabolical figure of the playwright or director inside the play, he abyssally evokes the 'monstrous birth' that the labour of the work will bring to light, thus articulating the narrative and dramatic structure of what is to come, not only on this particular occasion (this viewing, this reading) but also as the structural condition of that repeating machine called *Othello*. And at the same time, by this very gesture, he disarticulates it, burying the monster that has yet to appear. At what moment does the 'monstrous birth' in *Othello*, the 'monstrous birth' *of Othello*, arrive? Has anyone ever seen it?

Like Shakespeare's, Derrida's work shows a profound if paradoxical (singular and inventive) attachment to the normal. If deconstruction is monstrous, it is only with a view to 'disturbing the norms' ('ANU' 85), transforming the normal. For, as Derrida has also made clear, there are 'normal monstrosities' (SST 79), monstrosities of the normal. The challenge of his work — what makes it at once frightening and exhilarating — has to do with how it prompts us to rethink our conceptions of the world, and opens up new and extraordinary possibilities of writing and reading, thinking and doing.

Why, for example, write a piece of literary criticism or a philosophical essay that conforms to this or that kind of discourse or 'ism' (new criticism, new historicism, deconstructionism or whatever)? Derrida declares:

> Instead of giving in to normalizing and legitimating representations which iden-
> tify, recognize, and reduce everything too quickly, why not rather be interested
> in 'theoretical' monsters, in the monstrosities which announce themselves
> in theory, in the monsters who, beforehand, outdate and make comical all
> classifications or rhythms such as: after New Criticism comes an 'ism' and
> then a 'postism', and then again another 'ism', and today still another 'ism', etc.
> These last normalizations are themselves monstrous from the perspective of
> what happens in the most singular and inventive work and texts, in the most
> idiomatic writings; but these monstrosities are normal. They can be found
> everywhere.
>
> (SST 79)

Again, for anyone contemplating writing an 'academic' essay or book, this passage sketches a breathtaking sort of challenge. There is also here what might be called a characteristic inversion: Derrida's suggestion that we rethink the 'normal' as itself 'monstrous' corresponds, for example, to the kind of move he makes in that strange fragmentary text called 'Telepathy', when he wonders, not whether there is such a thing as 'telepathy' but, rather, whether *non*-telepathy is possible (see T 504).

JUSTICE

It perhaps did not require President George W. Bush to announce the beginning of the first war of the twenty-first century, in the wake of the terrorist attacks on the US in September 2001. In Derrida's terms the world was already at war. As he argues in *Specters of Marx* (1993), there is a 'war of messianic eschatologies' that has as its focus the 'appropriation of Jerusalem'. Derrida remarks: 'The war for the "appropriation of Jerusalem" is today the world war. It is happening everywhere, it is the world, it is today the singular figure of [the world's] being "out of joint"' (SM 58). At the Labour Party Conference in Brighton on 2 October 2001, the British Prime Minister Tony Blair gave a forceful speech concerned with the vision of a new world order, with a desire to 'reorder this world around us', in the wake of that 'turning point in history' called 'September 11'. In his concluding, notably infantilizing remarks, Blair asserted: 'Jews, Muslims and Christians are all children of Abraham. This is the moment to bring the faiths closer together in understanding of our common values and heritage, a source of unity and strength' (Blair 2001, 4–5).

For Derrida all of these faiths are founded on something monstrous. As he argues in the extraordinary work entitled *The Gift of Death* (1992), the story of Abraham, and in particular the story of Abraham and his willingness 'to put to death his beloved son', is precisely 'monstrous' (GD 67). Part of what makes the story of Abraham and Isaac monstrous, for Derrida, is 'the absence of women' (GD 75), the sense that 'the system of this sacrificial responsibility' appears to presuppose 'an exclusion or sacrifice of woman' (76). It is a father-and-son affair. More generally perhaps, it is monstrous to the extent that it figures 'the most common thing', 'the most common and everyday experience of responsibility' (67). Abraham's readiness to sacrifice his son is exemplary of every experience of responsibility that 'binds me to the other, to the other as other' (68).

The story of Abraham and Isaac conforms, in its singular fashion, to Derrida's contention that 'every other is completely other' (68: *tout autre est tout autre*: every other (one) is every (bit) other). Derrida's work prompts a rethinking of 'God' in this context, at the same time as a rethinking of prayer. If differance 'blocks every relationship to theology' (Pos 40), this (as we saw in Chapter 7) might be said to entail a rethinking of 'God' as in some sense always accompanied by the phrase 'for example': 'God, for example' (Diff 26). Thus, *for example*, Derrida has said: 'In every prayer there must be an address to the other as other; *for example* – I will say, at the risk of shocking – *God*' (H 110). In *The Gift of Death* he argues that Jerusalem is the site on, for or around which 'Isaac's sacrifice continues every day. Countless machines of death wage a war that has no front' (GD 70). (For a related example of Derrida's thinking in this context, we might consider his account of the 'monstrosity' of that 'political idiom' of racism known as 'apartheid' and the 'theologico-political discourse' on which it depended: see RLW 292, 296.)

From this brief discussion it may be evident that all of Derrida's work thus calls to be read as a kind of war literature, or philosophy of war, *at war*. As he has declared elsewhere, there is 'war and *polemos*' in 'every interpretation' (FL 999). His concern is with new ways of inheriting: as he has emphasized, 'inheritance is never a *given*, it is always a task' (SM 54). He is concerned with new ways of inheriting, questioning and perhaps transforming the logic of this monstrous story that is at the heart of these three monotheisms, at the 'essence' of 'Judeo–Christian–Islamic morality' (GD 64). In *Specters of Marx* and elsewhere, he describes this concern in terms of a 'messianism without religion', another thinking of 'the idea of justice' (SM 59). This involves an openness to a thinking of the future as the 'coming of the other', 'an entirely other that can no longer be confused with the God or the Man of ontotheology' (PIO 60–1). As a *yes* of 'unconditional welcome' (Hos 77), it engages an 'experience of the emancipatory promise' (SM 59).

At issue here is what binds deconstruction to 'another space for democracy' (SM 169), to the promise of the 'democracy to come'. In *Specters of Marx*, *Politics of Friendship* and elsewhere, Derrida has consistently argued that democracy never finally arrives, it is always to come. At the end of *Politics of Friendship* he writes:

> For democracy remains to come; this is its essence insofar as it remains: not only will it remain indefinitely perfectible, hence always insufficient and future, but, belonging to the time of the promise, it will always remain, in each of its future times, to come: even when there is democracy, it never exists, it is never present, it remains the theme of a non-presentable concept.
>
> (PF 306)

In this figure of 'the time of the promise', democracy and deconstruction are inextricably linked. There is, Derrida contends, 'no deconstruction without democracy, no democracy without deconstruction' (PF 105).

In a lecture that might now seem in certain details uncanny, as if clairvoyant, entitled 'Force of Law: The "Mystical Foundation of Authority"', given in October 1989 at the Cardozo Law School in Manhattan, Derrida speaks emphatically of the *place* where he is speaking, on Fifth Avenue, as being 'only a few blocks away from the inferno of injustice' (FL 997). In this lecture he calls for a sense of 'infinite justice' quite different from that monstrously invoked by the US Government in the wake of the terrorist attacks in September 2001. ('Infinite Justice', you may recall, was the name originally chosen for the US military operation launched in response to those attacks. Deeply offensive to Muslims – and to innumerable non-Muslims as well – this name was quickly dropped.) Derrida argues for 'a reinterpretation of the whole apparatus of boundaries within which a history and a culture have been able to confine their criteriology' for a concept of justice. Deconstruction, he says, is 'already engaged by this infinite demand of justice, for justice' (FL 955). It is concerned rather with 'the sense of a responsibility without limits, and so necessarily excessive, incalculable, before memory' (953).

World war continues. Deconstruction wages war on everything that seeks to 'maintain an effective inequality as monstrous as that which prevails today, to a greater extent than ever in the history of humanity' (SM 85). Deconstruction is 'mad about justice' (FL 965), Derrida declares. His concern to construe responsibility and justice 'without limits' goes hand in hand with the commitment to 'a profound transformation . . . of international law'. As he argues in *Specters of Marx*: 'international law should extend and diversify its field to include, if at least it is to be consistent with the idea of democracy and of human rights it proclaims, the *worldwide* economic and social field' (SM 84). Like deconstruction and democracy, justice entails a sense of the 'to come': 'justice', says Derrida, 'is yet, to come, *à venir*' (FL 969). In its encounter with the undecidable, aporia and incalculability, justice concerns a thinking of the 'experience of the impossible' (947), of a 'gift without exchange' (965). (I shall say more about the notion of the gift in Chapter 11.) All of which is not to suggest that justice, any more than deconstruction or democracy, can wait. As Derrida insists in 'Force of Law': 'justice, however unpresentable it may be, doesn't wait. It is that which must not wait' (FL 967).

10

SECRET LIFE

In an earlier chapter ('The most interesting thing in the world'), I suggested that 'good' literary criticism always involves a certain inhabiting of the literary. This critical inhabiting entails an attempt to sign or countersign, attest to or vouch for what is distinctive and provoking about the literary text that is being read. If the literary work is an act (and this is a consistent affirmation in Derrida's writings), so too is the work of literary criticism. As Derrida puts it: ' "Good" literary criticism, the only worthwhile kind, implies an act, a literary signature or counter-signature, an inventive experience of language, *in* language, an inscription of the act of reading in the field of the text that is read' (TSICL 52). It is a matter of the singular. In the following pages I will focus on the importance of the notion of the singular in Derrida's work, in an attempt to clarify a cluster of related issues: the signature, the idiom, autobiography and the secret.

IT ONLY HAPPENS TO ME

Every literary work is singular, and every reading of such a work is singular. This singularity of the work has to do with the unique idiom, style and signature of the author. Everyone writes – and reads – differently, in their own, singular fashion. Derrida's argument about singularity can be broadened out. Everyone has their own way of doing, thinking, feeling or experiencing things: it may be a question of how you choose to pose – or how you find yourself posing – for a photograph (TNON 200–1); it might be the 'singular situation' of having a conversation with someone, on a certain fine day, for example, with *the sea on my right* (TS 70). 'It only happens to me' (C 305), as Derrida summarizes it in his strange autobiographical work entitled 'Circumfession'.

This singularity, however, entails a double-bind. Derrida puts the paradox in a nutshell: 'The desire for the idiom – nothing is less idiomatic' (SF 360). The singular is in fact always bound up with the general. An 'absolutely pure singularity . . . would not be available for reading': in order to be 'readable', what is singular (a wink, a word, a sentence, a novel or philosophical treatise) has to participate in 'the genre, the type, the context, meaning, the conceptual generality of meaning' (TSICL 68). The uniqueness of the singular, of one's own idiom, one's own signature, is in fact always already compromised, divided, haunted. Thus, Derrida argues, while it is 'usually interpreted as one's very own mark, [the signature] is instead what I cannot appropriate, cannot make my own' (TS 85).

The 'desire for idiom' is an endless desire, for the idiomatic is 'a property that one cannot appropriate; it signs you without belonging to you' (U 119). Derrida proposes another thinking of the proper, proper name, property and appropriation in general. All of these 'proper' terms relate to the Latin *proprius*, meaning 'own'. All of Derrida's work can be characterized by a concern to question and rethink the 'ownness' of the 'proper'. As he has put it: 'I do not believe appropriation to be possible in general' (ATED 141). The work is singular, but what goes for the uniqueness of a Shakespeare sonnet also goes for a Rembrandt or a personal cheque: forgery is 'always possible' (ATED 133). As Derrida (or someone very like him) has said: 'the possibility of the forgery always defines the very structure of the event called signature' (BB 25).

The preoccupation with notions of idiom and signature is perhaps most fully explored in his astonishing little book on the French poet Francis Ponge, entitled *Signsponge* (S). This preoccupation goes to the heart of Derrida's fascination with literature and poetry. It is also one reason why his work really annoys some philosophers (and non-philosophers too). At least in traditional terms, philosophical discourse is not supposed to be about the philosopher's 'desire for idiom', about his (or, less commonly, her) desire to leave a singular and distinctive mark, to stamp his (or her) name on the history of philosophy. Yet, as Derrida repeatedly shows, notions of singularity, idiom and signature are as crucial and as illuminating for thinking about philosophy or literary criticism as about literature or poetry.

A name, such as 'Jacques Derrida', is supposed to be proper insofar as it is outside the semantic economy of a language: its referent is unique, the one and only Jacques Derrida. There might be several people called Jacques Derrida, but for each one of them the proper name is felt to be properly and uniquely his. No doubt you will have supposed that when I have been talking about 'Jacques Derrida' I have been referring to the same one every time. 'I do not seek to establish any kind of authenticity' (LI 55): this might be taken as a watchword for all of Derrida's work. His concern is rather with pointing up the uncanniness, the unmasterability, the experiences of aporia, double bind and undecidability as regards the related notions of proper name, the proper and property, the signature and singularity.

The 'desire for idiom' thus flits about his texts in explicit, ironic, sometimes humorous, sometimes surreal ways. In *Glas* (1974), in the 'Envois' section of *The Post Card* (1980) and elsewhere, his initials, 'JD', are deployed in reverse form as '*déjà*' (DJ, 'already'). A logic of reversal or reversibility, and of the 'always already', is *always already* inscribed in JD's name. This DJ/JD stages a sort of cryptic, collapsing mime of deconstruction, insofar as this latter involves the overturning, reversal and rewriting of conceptual oppositions and hierarchies (see Pos 41–2), a logic of life, thinking, speech, writing etc. as *always already haunted* (see, in particular, SM).

Derrida's post cards (the 'envois') in *The Post Card* also work with bizarre deformations of his name, such as '*j'accepte*' ['I accept', playing on 'Jacques accepts'] (E 34), as well as

der – a sort of *derformed* German 'the' –

id – immediately Derrida's id as much (and as little) as Freud's, or perhaps Coleridge's, or indeed the 'id' or 'idiom' of anyone –

da – 'there' in German, i.e. not here but at a distance, absent, gone, dead, as in '*fort/da*', an allusion to Freud's account, in *Beyond the Pleasure Principle*, of a child's supposed coming-to-terms with the absence of his mother (see Freud 1984, 269–338) – and

derrière les rideaux – Derrida 'behind the curtains': is he there or isn't he? Who, he? Derrida the magician, the disappearing act, the name as – empty? – secret.

(See E 78)

There is a sort of aesthetic or literary playfulness in this, but it is of a strange kind, irreducible to the merely 'aesthetic' or 'literary' or 'play-ful'. If it is narcissistic, it would be in terms of what Derrida has called 'a new understanding of narcissism' (see RI), and in particular in terms of what he refers to as the 'double-bind or double-faced logics' of narcis-sism, namely that 'the more there is, the less there is' (E 52). Of the phrase '*derrière les rideaux*', for example, he has commented that, in the desire to 'lose one's name', by 'disarticulating it', by turning it into a common noun, one also wins it: it is a scene of double bind in which 'one loses what one wins and wins what one loses' (EO 76–7). The proper is proper only on condition of being no longer proper.

There is a funny moment in *Monty Python and the Holy Grail* (director, Terry Gilliam, 1974) when a roughly spoken Scottish laird is trying to get his feeble, theatrically effeminate son to pull himself together. He gestures vigorously towards the vast estate that lies beyond the windows of his castle and loudly declares: 'One day, son, all of *this* will be *yours!*' The son looks towards the window and says, in a whimpering sort of way: 'What, the *curtains?*' This exchange about inheriting curtains is perhaps helpful here as a means of foregrounding the role of the father in relation to the proper. As Derrida analyses it in *Glas* (G), 'Le facteur de la vérité' (FV), *Signsponge* and elsewhere, the workings of the proper are intimately linked to phallogocentrism, in other words to everything in western culture that ties proper meaning, authority and presence (in a word, the Word: *logos*) to the imaginary and symbolic power of the phallus.

Such is the effect of the name of the father, as Derrida suggests in his account of Juliet's 'implacable analysis' (AC 427) of the proper name in Shakespeare's play. Juliet's question is not only 'O Romeo, Romeo, wherefore art thou Romeo?' but also, perhaps more incisively: 'What's Montague?' It is the son who carries the name, Derrida stresses, and 'not at all . . . the daughter who has never been put in charge of it' (AC 430). It is the so-called family name (the 'Montague'), not the forename ('Romeo'), that determines the tragedy. Everything comes down to the impossibility inscribed in Juliet's imploring him: 'O, be some other name!' (see *Romeo and Juliet*, 2.1.75 ff). Juliet's 'terrible lucidity', in Derrida's reading, consists in her understanding of 'the *double bind*, which ties a son to the name of his father'. Romeo Montague 'can only live if he asserts himself in a singular fashion, without his inherited name. But the writing of this name, which he has not written himself ("Had I it written, I would tear the word" [2.1.99]), constitutes him in his very being' (AC 430). Derrida is not here dealing explicitly with the notion of the signature, though Romeo's reference to the essential non-ownership of the writing of his name indicates the essential deadliness that haunts any such writing. As Derrida asks in *Spurs*: 'What, after all, is handwriting?' (Sp 127). At some level, when one writes one's name, whether or not it is supposed to be a signature, death is always there: it's always curtains.

One may want to sign one's work, in and with one's so-called proper name. One may want one's writing to be recognized as one's own and nobody else's. But, as John Llewelyn has succinctly phrased it, 'the author's signature . . . alienates as it identifies' (Llewelyn 1986, 71). The idiomatic is the commonplace. As I suggested in the opening pages of this book, to love one's name is to love what is not one's own (see AI 219); one is always a stranger to one's name (see AC 427). Or as Derrida puts it in one of the 'Envois': 'you will never be your name, you never have been, even when, and especially when you have answered to it. The name is made to do without the life of the bearer, and is therefore always somewhat the name of someone dead' (E 39).

Derrida analyses this in a reading of the poetry of Francis Ponge: 'the signature has to remain and disappear at the same time, remain in order to disappear, or disappear in order to remain' (S 56). Elsewhere in *Signsponge*, he notes:

The proper name, in its aleatoriness, should have no meaning and should spend itself in immediate reference. But the chance or the misery of its arbitrary character (always other in each case) is that its inscription in language always affects it with a potential for meaning, and for no longer being proper once it has a meaning.

(S 118)

It is a question of the necessary role of the aleatory, the necessity of chance. It is not Derrida's fault or choice that his name can seem to be glimpsed '*derrière les rideaux*' [behind the curtains], any more than it is down to me that the letters of the word 'Royle' are anagrammatically dispersed in the 'aleatory' or that among the senses of the homophonic verb to 'roil' (especially in North American English) are: 'to roam about', 'play', 'irritate', 'shake up', to 'de-sediment' or in other words *to deconstruct*. As Derrida has remarked: 'Obviously this is not something one can decide: one doesn't disseminate or play with one's name. The very structure of the proper name sets this process in motion' (EO 76). Far from wishing to pretend that one can or should ignore the 'desire for the idiom', Derrida is in a sense interested in nothing else. His thinking is impelled, he says, by the 'dream' of an 'idiomatic writing'. The 'purity' of this dreamed-of writing is 'inaccessible', but still he hearkens towards it. This is why he feels his ' "first" desire' led him toward literature rather than toward philosophy. This dream or desire is, he says, 'something that literature makes room for better than philosophy' (U 118).

As works such as *Glas* and 'Envois' make clear, one never finally, completely signs something, leaving a mark or nick that would be uniquely and purely one's own. This, as I hope to demonstrate in more detail in the following chapter, is partly what draws Derrida to the question and experience of poetry. As he declares at the end of the short text entitled 'Che cos'è la poesia?' (the Italian phrase meaning 'What is poetry?' or, more literally, 'What thing is poetry?'): 'A poem, I never sign(s) it' (Che 237). A poem would perhaps be the kind of text or experience that most sharply, most traumatically engages this impossibility, this unsignable desire that appears to you only in flashes of madness. All of Derrida's work, however, is impelled by this desire for the idiomatic. As he has put it, the idiomatic

> only appears to the other and it never comes back to you except in flashes of madness that bring together life and death, that bring you together dead and alive at the same time. You dream, it's unavoidable, about the invention of a language or of a song that would be yours, not the attributes of a 'self', rather the accentuated paraph, that is, the musical signature, of your most unreadable history.
>
> (U 119)

You are driven, he suggests, by an idiomatic desire, a desire for the idiomatic that links the experience of the signature with that of song or music. This experience is impossible (and we might recall here, once again, Derrida's 'least bad definition' of 'deconstruction', as the 'experience of the impossible' [Aft 200]) – but this doesn't put an end to the 'dream' or 'flashes of madness'. On the contrary, they are what start you off and keep you going.

SECRET PASSAGEWAYS

All of this leads us to a topic that has pervaded the pages of this book but that has perhaps not been explicitly discussed, namely the secret. The notion of the secret is at issue as soon as we start reflecting on what 'only happens to me' (it must be, in some sense, secret); on the cryptic nature of the desire for idiom (what is this 'inaccessible' purity of the idiom?); on the obscure 'place' of death in the name. A few moments ago, in the context of Derrida's '*derrière les rideaux*', I evoked the notion of the name as '(empty?) secret'. In his short book entitled *Aporias* Derrida writes:

> *Death* is always the name of a secret, since it signs the irreplaceable singularity. It puts forth the public name, the common name of a secret, the common name of the proper name without name. . . . [L]anguage about death is nothing but the long history of a secret society, neither public nor private, semi-private, semi-public, on the border between the two.
>
> (A 74)

In speaking of 'death' as the 'name of a secret' Derrida seeks to trace a space for a thinking of the secret no longer in terms of what can in principle be revealed, but rather in terms of what remains '*absolutely indecipherable*' (GT 152). As he declares, in aphoristic fashion, in the essay 'Passions: "An Oblique Offering"': '*There is something secret*. But it does not conceal itself' (POO 21).

In this context we might note that there is perhaps nothing essentially human about the secret or secrecy. The notion of 'death' as secret calls for another thinking of the human and the animal, and of the human as animal. As Derrida emphatically argues in *Aporias*:

> animals have a very significant relation to death . . . even if they have neither a relation to death nor to the 'name' of death as such, nor, by the same token, to the other as such, to the purity as such of the alterity of the other as such. But neither does man, that is precisely the point!
>
> (A 76)

One can call this secret by any name, but 'it remains secret under all names' (POO 21). There is something 'absolute' about it (see POO 22–5). It is 'heterogeneous to the hidden', he argues: it 'simply exceeds the play of veiling/unveiling' (POO 21). He describes this experience of the secret very well in an interview in 1994:

> Clearly, the most tempting figure for this absolute/secret is death, that which has a relation to death, that which is carried off by death – that which is thus life itself. Now, it is true that the relation to death is a privileged dimension of this experience of the secret, *but I imagine that an immortal would have the same experience.* . . . . Fundamentally, everything I attempt to do, think, teach and write has its raison d'être, spur, calling and appeal in this secret, which interminably disqualifies any effort one can make to determine it.
>
> (TS 58)

He goes on to say that this is a secret 'that we *speak* of but are unable to *say*'. 'It is the sharing of what is not shared', he says: 'we know in common that we have nothing in common' (TS 58).

Derrida's notion of the secret might be elaborated in all sorts of directions: it haunts every word, every name, 'at every instant' (POO 21). For the moment, however, permit me merely to indicate three connected paths or passageways.

First, autobiography. 'The autobiographical is the locus of the secret' (TS 57). In other words, we might try (along with Derrida, in 'Circumfession' [C], 'A Silkworm of One's Own' [SOO] and elsewhere) to re-elaborate autobiography as this space of the secret. It would be a question of autobiographical discourse not as the place where one's inner self is revealed, where sexual intimacies or cupboards crammed with skeletons are opened up to the public eye, but as the place for the experience of the impossible, an engagement with what we can speak of but cannot say, with a secrecy that is 'heterogeneous to the hidden'. My life is a secret life. What 'only happens to me' has to do with what I can speak of but cannot say, with an otherness or alterity that can never be present, perceived or experienced. We might be tempted to name the secret as 'death' but, Derrida suggests, we might just as reasonably call it 'life, existence, trace' (POO 24). The autobiographical is inextricably 'heterothanatographical' (SF 273): writing one's life is a matter of '*life death*' (see SF 292 and passim).

Second, politics and religion. Especially in work published since the early 1990s (GD, SM, PF, FK), Derrida has sought to analyse, question and transform some of the profound links between politics and religion. The notion of the secret is crucial in this context. He notes that 'if a right to the secret is not maintained, we are in a totalitarian space' (TS 59). In conventional terms, there can be no democracy without secrets (whether this be the secrecy of what is going on in one's head or the secrecy of the ballot-box). Derrida claims to have 'a taste for the secret' and this leads him to entwine a conventional with a deconstructive notion of secret, while insisting that 'the two are heterogeneous' (59). The entwining has to do with the notion of belonging: 'Belonging – the fact of avowing one's belonging, of putting in common – be it family, nation, tongue – spells the loss of the secret' (59). Derrida's declaration of a 'New International' (part of the sub-title of *Specters of Marx*) involves the affirmation of a 'link of affinity' that is 'almost secret' while at the same time insistently at odds with notions of belonging: it is a link 'without status, without title . . . without party, without country, without national community (International before, across, and beyond any national determination), without co-citizenship, without common belonging to a class' (SM 85). In *Specters of Marx* and elsewhere, Derrida's thinking of democracy (or what he calls the 'democracy to come') entails a sense of promise, 'a messianism without religion' (SM 59) and a construal of the secret in non-religious terms. He is guided by a thinking of the secret as what 'does not belong' and is 'for no one' (GD 92). This is a matter of 'demystification' (GD 102). 'The secret is not mystical' (POO 21), as he asserts in the essay 'Passions': its strange 'locus' precedes and exceeds that of religious revelation or revealability.

Third, literature. In *Given Time: 1. Counterfeit Money*, in a reading of a prose poem entitled 'Counterfeit Money' ('La fausse monnaie') by Charles Baudelaire (1821–67), Derrida focuses on what he regards as 'the secret *of* literature', which is also 'a secret whose possibility assures the possibility of literature'. He describes this as consisting in 'the altogether bare device of being-two-to-speak' (GT 153). It is perhaps easiest to envisage this in terms of what is conventionally called third-person narrative fiction, especially the kind with a so-called omniscient (or, better perhaps, telepathic) narrator. An example here would be the shopping list in Bowen's *The Death of the Heart* which I discussed earlier (in Chapter 7): as soon as an author or narrator presents us with a sort of secret knowledge, in other words with what is (or is not) going on in the mind and body of someone else (most obviously, of a character in the text), there is this 'altogether bare device' that Derrida is talking about. Another example would be James Thurber's whimsical story 'The Secret Life of Walter Mitty', a third-person narrative which, in presenting the protagonist's so-called 'secret life', lays bare this very secrecy. Conversely, in the case of a first-person narrative: as soon as a text presents us with an 'I' who is in some way or other distinguished from the author of that text, we are in the strange domain of literature. This being-two-to-speak (or, we might add, being-two-to-write, being-two-to-think and being-two-to-feel) conducts us towards the secret of literature. It is the strange, cryptic thing that makes literature possible.

11

POETRY BREAK

There is no poetry without poetry break. Such will perhaps have been the subject of Samuel Taylor Coleridge's *Kubla Khan* (1797). In the following pages I propose to use Coleridge's great poem as a point of reference and illustration for an account of a number of topics that are, I believe, crucially helpful towards an understanding of Derrida's work: unreadability, drugs, the poematic and the gift. Here is the poem:

In Xanadu did Kubla Khan
A stately pleasure-dome decree,
Where Alph, the sacred river, ran
Through caverns measureless to man
  Down to a sunless sea.   [5]
So twice five miles of fertile ground
With walls and towers were girdled round;
And here were gardens bright with sinuous rills
Where blossomed many an incense-bearing tree;
And here were forests ancient as the hills,   [10]
And folding sunny spots of greenery.

But oh, that deep romantic chasm which slanted
Down the green hill athwart a cedarn cover!
A savage place, as holy and enchanted

As e'er beneath a waning moon was haunted   [15]
By woman wailing for her demon-lover!
And from this chasm, with ceaseless turmoil seething,
As if this earth in fast thick pants were breathing,
A mighty fountain momently was forced
Amid whose swift half-intermitted burst   [20]
Huge fragments vaulted like rebounding hail,
Or chaffy grain beneath the thresher's flail!
And mid these dancing rocks at once and ever,
It flung up momently the sacred river.
Five miles meandering with a mazy motion   [25]
Through wood and dale the sacred river ran,
Then reached the caverns measureless to man
And sank in tumult to a lifeless ocean.
And mid this tumult Kubla heard from far
Ancestral voices prophesying war!   [30]

   The shadow of the dome of pleasure
   Floated midway on the waves,
   Where was heard the mingled measure
   From the fountain and the caves;
It was a miracle of rare device,   [35]
A sunny pleasure-dome with caves of ice!

   A damsel with a dulcimer
   In a vision once I saw:
   It was an Abyssinian maid
   And on her dulcimer she played,   [40]
   Singing of Mount Abora.
   Could I revive within me
   Her symphony and song,
   To such a deep delight 'twould win me
That with music loud and long,   [45]
I would build that dome in air,
That sunny dome, those caves of ice!
And all who heard should see them there,
And all should cry, 'Beware, beware!
His flashing eyes, his floating hair!   [50]
Weave a circle round him thrice,
And close your eyes with holy dread –

For he on honey-dew hath fed
And drank the milk of Paradise.'

(in Wu 1998, 523–4)

UNREADABILITY

As clearly as any other poem written in English in the past 200 years or
so, *Kubla Khan* might seem to corroborate Derrida's notion of the 'enigmatic kinship between . . . nuclear waste and the "masterpiece"' (Bio
845). It 'resists erosion' (845), to recall his phrase in 'Biodegradables',
which is to say also that it resists being read at the same time as it
demands our reading. It is compellingly unreadable, it is fascinating *on
account of its unreadability*. Derrida's work consistently draws attention
to a notion of the unreadable that is not opposed to the readable.
'Unreadability', he argues, 'does not arrest reading, does not leave it
paralyzed in the face of an opaque surface: rather, it starts reading and
writing and translation moving again' (LO 116). 'The unreadability of
the text' entails what Derrida has called 'the impossibility of acceding
to its proper significance and its possibly inconsistent content, which it
jealously keeps back' (B 211). This, as he makes clear in the essay
'Before the Law', is the law of reading and writing.

The 'proper significance' of the text is deferred, but not until some
future moment when all is finally revealed. Neither is it a matter of
saying that the 'proper significance' is simply and categorically deferred
forever, as if in effect it wouldn't have made any difference whether it
were deferred or not. This would be to deny or efface the disruptive,
constitutive, insistent strangeness of the force of deferral that is going
on right now, effecting what Derrida has called the singularity of a
here and now 'without present' (TS 12–13). Rather, this 'proper significance' is marked by death. It is, in his phrase, 'deferred forever till
death' (B 205). In other words, it is a question of the irreplaceably
singular: your death, or my death. It is a matter of reading as an experience (in and of deferral) that 'only happens to me' (C 305).

Coleridge's *Kubla Khan* is an inexhaustibly cryptic, secretive text – in
ways that engage with questions of autobiography, politics, religion and
literature, among so many others. It leaves us, on every new reading
(and there are hundreds of published readings of the poem, not to
mention the countless other, unpublished readings), with a sense of 'the
impossibility of acceding to its proper significance'. Why is it called

Kubla Khan? What is the poem about? What is this 'miracle of rare device'? Who is the 'damsel' and who the 'I'? And who are those that 'cry'? What is the 'honey-dew' and 'milk of paradise'? We cannot arrive at conclusive, conversation-stopping answers to these questions. Rather they are questions that open on to the experience of what Derrida calls 'the absolute inviolability of the secret' (GT 153). What is cryptic or secret about *Kubla Khan* is not something that could one day, in princi- ple, be 'explained away', 'solved', 'revealed'. It is rather a matter of a 'superficial' yet 'inaccessible' unreadability. To recall Derrida's phras- ing: '*There is something secret*. But it does not conceal itself' (POO 21). Or as he puts it in *Given Time*: 'the readability of the text is structured by the unreadability of the secret' (GT 152).

Any text might bear witness to this unreadability. Correspondingly, there is no essence of literature: any text *might* be read as literary. But if there is something exemplary about literature, it perhaps has to do with the notion of 'possibly inconsistent content', with the secret or cryptic strangeness of a consistent inconsistency whereby 'literature . . . always is, says, does something other, something other than itself, an itself which moreover is only that, something other than itself' (POO 33). What makes a text 'great', in Derrida's terms, has to do with its capacity for 'inducing meaning without being exhausted by meaning', for inducing a sense of the 'incomprehensibly elliptical' or 'secret', in particular by 'join[ing] the universal wealth of the "message"' to the 'finally unreadable', 'unintelligible singularity' of a signature. Derrida's concern is with a notion of the work (in particular a work of literature or philosophy) as an 'irreplaceable singularity' which entwines the readable and the unreadable and thus comes to figure a 'singular impro- priety' that cannot be appropriated by anyone, whether reader or presumed author (see Bio 845).

Coleridge's *Kubla Khan* is unlike any other poem, even as it is rec- ognizable *as* a poem. It is unique. To recall the first of the axiomatic beliefs that govern a reading, as Derrida outlines it in 'Before the Law': a text 'has its own identity, singularity and unity' (B 184). As with the example of Kafka's text ('Vor dem Gesetz'), we presuppose that *Kubla Khan* is 'unique and self-identical' and 'exist[s] as an original version incorporated in its birthplace within the [English] language' (B 185). It figures as an irreplaceable singularity. But this irreplaceable singularity is always already compromised. I have just indicated as much by noting that *Kubla Khan* is *recognized* as a poem and by substituting its exemplarity with that of Kafka's text. As Derrida has observed in a reading of Blanchot's 'The Instant of My Death' (1994), the logic according to which 'the example is not substitutable' entails an aporia: 'this irreplace-ability must be exemplary, that is, replaceable' (Dem 41). The context of his remark is that of bearing witness. But the singularity of Derrida's remark is itself substitutable: to bear witness is to read, to be able to read, to be called upon to be responsible to and for reading. What he says about witnessing is also a description of what happens when we read a poem, such as *Kubla Khan*: we are called upon to bear witness, to countersign.

What makes *Kubla Khan* such a haunting, powerful 'singular impro-priety' has to do, perhaps, with the way in which it figures *as* an irreplaceable singularity while also, at the same time, being a poem *about* irreplaceable singularity. It is concerned with a singular 'vision', witnessed only 'once': 'A damsel with a dulcimer/In a vision *once* I saw'. The revival or recurrence of this vision would apparently enable the 'I' of the poem to 'build' in sound, synaesthetically, to build 'with music loud and long' and amid what Derrida might call 'flashes of madness' ('Beware! Beware!/His flashing eyes, his floating hair!'), to build precisely the 'sunny dome' and 'caves of ice' that the poem has already evoked and effectively constructed in its dream of words. There is supplementarity at the source. The dream of words that is the poem thus inscribes the very replaceability of this irreplaceably singular 'vision'. The singular 'vision' of the 'damsel with a dulcimer' is already an echo or repetition of the bizarre sub-title of the poem, accompanying its first publication: '*Kubla Khan: or A Vision in a Dream*' (see Wu 1998, 522). Is the irreplaceable 'vision' *in* the poem, or is it *the poem itself*, or are both vision and poem in *another vision*, the vision of 'a Dream'?

DRUGS

Perhaps the most celebrated, even notorious aspect of Coleridge's *Kubla Khan* has to do with its drugs link. This is the canonical English poem illus-trating the configuration of poetry or poetic inspiration and drugs. As someone who is not a regular opium-eater I should confess that, in my experience of teaching this poem in various seminars over a number of years, I am struck by how consistently this topic has reared its slightly crazed head in the form of a psychobiographical 'argument' (which of course is never an argument exactly, but rather a nebulous hypothesizing) that Coleridge was 'on opium' when he wrote this poem, that this is what the poem is all about and that that is in effect all that needs to be said. *Kubla Khan*: opium-reverie, end of story. I would like briefly to explore in a little more detail how we might think about these issues in the light of Derrida's work.

In his 1816 preface to the poem, Coleridge does of course refer to 'an anodyne' (i.e. opium: see Wu 1998, 522) taken just prior to the sleep that brought the vision that brought the poem to him. The evocations of 'honey-dew' and 'milk of paradise' (ll.53–4) likewise leave us in no doubt that *Kubla Khan* is indeed profoundly a poem *about* intoxication and drugs. But what are drugs? This is the question that Derrida discusses in a fascinating 1989 interview published in English as 'The Rhetoric of Drugs' (RD). In this interview we can see Derrida carrying out a characteristically singular and exhilarating 'experiment', namely to contextualize and analyse what is conventionally understood by the term 'drugs' and proceed to submit it to what he has called 'unbounded generalization' (TTP 40) while submitting himself, in this process, to a 'trip' of sorts, to the singular, aleatory 'trip' of speaking or writing. As I suggested earlier in this book (in the chapter on 'the supplement'), in a sense this is what he does again and again in his work, though always differently, depending on the 'term' (or 'key idea') in question. He seeks to disturb and deform the 'accredited, authorized relationship between a word and a concept, between a trope and what one had every interest to consider to be an unshiftable primary sense, a proper, literal or current usage' (TTP 40–1).

In the case of the discussion of drugs, this entails establishing that 'there are no drugs "in nature"' (RD 229). What this means is that *there are no non-drugs either*. Anything *might be* a drug. As Derrida puts it: 'We will always have unclassified or unclassifiable supplements of drugs or narcotics. Basically everyone has his [or her] own' (RD 245). Thus he offers what is perhaps his most concisely formulated proposition regarding the unbounded generalization in this context: 'Every phantasmatic organization, whether collective or individual, is the invention of a drug, or of a rhetoric of drugs, be it aphrodisiac or not' (RD 247). He foregrounds the crucial role of language and especially performative speech acts in 'the regime of the concept [of drugs]' (229), starting out with the 'diction' in 'addiction' (from the Latin *dīcere*, 'to declare', 'to say'). In doing so, he is especially attentive to the relations between drugs and literature, drugs and poetry. There are striking correspondences between the worlds of fiction or poetry and the world of drugs, in particular as regards the sense of a sort of dreaminess or what he elsewhere describes as 'a *suspended* relation to meaning and reference' (TSICL 48).

The world of drugs, Derrida suggests, is 'a world of simulacrum and fiction' (RD 235–6). (For two rather different accounts of Derrida, literature and the 'rhetoric of drugs' in this context, see Ronell 1992 and Boothroyd in Royle 2000.) The 'question of drugs', Derrida asserts, can indeed be regarded as 'the great question of truth' (RD 235). Recalling his analysis of the *pharmakon* ('drug', 'poison', 'remedy', etc.) in 'Plato's Pharmacy' (see PP 70 ff), he implicitly brings these different worlds together in proposing that, for Plato, 'writing is not only a drug, it is a game, *paideia*, and a bad game if it is no longer ruled by a concern for philosophical truth' (RD 234). At issue here is the notion of what might nowadays be called the writer's 'freedom of speech' as including 'a certain irresponsibility', and even a 'duty of irresponsibility' (TSICL 38). Derrida's point, both in 'Plato's Pharmacy' and elsewhere, is that one cannot simply and categorically separate *pharmakon* as 'remedy' from *pharmakon* as 'poison'. As we saw in our discussion of shopping lists (in Chapter 7), the *pharmakon* of writing can aid *and* efface memory: writing can be a way of remembering but also of forgetting. The sense and value of a *pharmakon* entails an experience of undecidability.

Writing is essentially 'a wandering' (RD 234). Writing is in some respects perhaps what is always given over to the other and what always comes from the other. It is in this context that Derrida explores the importance of the idea of what he calls 'figures of dictation', that is to say

> the experience of the other (of the being-given-over-to-the-other, of the being prey to the other, of quasi-possession) that commands a certain writing, perhaps all writing, even the most masterful (gods, the daemon, the muses, inspiration, and so forth).
>
> (RD 238)

In other words, the question of drugs in *Kubla Khan* is indissociably bound up with the experience of writing. It is not a matter of vainly speculating on the relative importance or unimportance of the role of Coleridge's opium-consumption in the composition of the poem, but of acknowledging a 'rhetoric of drugs', and a power of drugs, in its very writing and reading.

It is not only a question of how the poem figures dictation and desire in the song of the 'Abyssinian maid' (the abyssal-Abyssinian song that is identified with the experience of feeding on honey-dew and drinking the milk of paradise) but also of how the poem itself dictates, commands or decrees a kind of addictive reading or desire in the reader. Indeed, rather as if he were secretly mainlining *Kubla Khan* as he is speaking, Derrida declares: 'We should ask ourselves whether drug addiction consists simply and essentially in receiving and taking in, rather than in "expressing" and pushing outside, for example in a certain form of speaking or of singing' (RD 245). At this point it might indeed be apposite to reconsider the opening words of this book in which I suggested, apparently confidently, that 'Derrida' is not the name of some high-energy drink.

THE POEMATIC

Love is the drug, for Derrida. Deconstruction, he suggests, 'never proceeds without love' ('ANU' 83); or more succinctly, 'deconstruction is love' (see Royle 1995, 140). As he makes clear in the little hedgehog-like text entitled 'Che cos'è la poesia?', at the heart of poetry there is love or more precisely an 'I love you by heart'. This is the condition of the poem or of what he calls 'the poematic experience' (Che 231). 'Che cos'è la poesia?' is merely a few pages long, yet it is perhaps one of Derrida's most remarkable texts. If, as Peggy Kamuf notes, he always 'works to abolish the distance between what he is writing *about* . . . and what his writing is *doing*' (DRBB 221), 'Che cos'è la poesia?' is among his most lapidary performatives or perverformatives (see E 136). This is in keeping with the conception of poetry towards which the text motions you: 'a poem must be brief, elliptical by vocation, whatever may be its objective or apparent expanse' (225). Not only does this little essay appear to do a lot by saying very little, but it also seems unusual (even for Derrida!) in terms of the extent to which it manages to *perform perversely*, that is to say to generate new and quite unforeseen effects every time you read it. 'You' here, I must add, is not mine: Derrida's poematic text is itself written in the second person ('you'), indeed in the intimate '*tu*' form.

Quite exceptionally in the context of Derrida's œuvre, 'Che cos'è la poesia?' does not offer a specific detailed reading of any other text or writer. Rather he focuses in provoking ways on the phrase 'demon of the heart', apparently anonymous yet in quotation marks. Unattributed, the poem is 'this "demon of the heart" [*démon du coeur*]' (234/5). Perhaps playing (a little maniacally) on the demon in demonstration (*démon/démontrer*), he tells you that this demon 'had to be demonstrated' (236/7). Itself a 'demon of the heart', Derrida's text suggests a logic of the demonized heart, demonized love, the work of a 'demon-lover'. 'The poetic . . . would be that which you desire to learn, but from and of the other and under dictation, by heart' (227). To love a poem is to want to have it in your heart, to learn it by heart, to be unable to help yourself wanting to learn it by heart. But Derrida also radicalizes this formulation by saying: 'I call a poem that very thing that teaches the heart, invents the heart' (231). Love is inseparable from the poematic.

To learn by heart is, in French, *apprendre par coeur*: the verb *apprendre* carries the sense of 'to teach' and 'to hear', as well as 'to learn'. Derrida's text also evokes a sense of taking: like the English verb 'to apprehend', *apprendre* suggests a taking hold of, an appropriation. In English we might think of the phrase 'to have by heart'. You want to have the poem by heart. A poem that you love says: 'I am *a* dictation . . . copy me down, guard and keep me' (223). In other words, a drug, a foreign body wanting to be inside you, the poem says *take me*: 'Eat, drink, swallow my letter, carry it, transport it in you' (229). Let me be your honey-dew. But the poem is not for the having. This ' "demon of the heart" never gathers itself together, rather it loses itself and gets off the track (delirium or mania)' (235). The 'by heart' is at once the way of love and exposure to 'a certain exteriority of the automaton' (231): to learn by heart is always contaminated and haunted by the deadly machine-like 'to learn by rote'.

The poem is the impossible experience of an apocalyptic desire. 'Che cos'è la poesia?' decrees that it is necessary to break with poetry, with everything that might have been gathered in or under the name 'poetry': it is necessary to 'set fire to the library of poetics. The unicity of the poem depends on this condition. You must celebrate, you have to commemorate amnesia, savagery' (233). In this way Derrida traces a radically unfamiliar, provocatively idiomatic notion of poetry. The poem is said to be 'a stranger to all production, especially to creation' (233). It is rather a sort of passion, a suffering of chance, a 'wounding' (233). The poem is not even a matter of language in any conventional sense. 'Our poem', Derrida declares, 'does not hold still within names, nor even within words': it is a 'thing beyond languages, even if it sometimes happens that it recalls itself in language' (229). 'You will call a poem from now on a certain passion of the singular mark, the signature that repeats its dispersion' (235), he remarks. The poem is, to adopt a phrase from elsewhere, 'more intimate with one than one is oneself' (SM 172). The desire to learn by heart is not something that comes *after* the identification of the 'I': rather, 'the *I* is only at the coming of this desire' (Che 237). 'In Xanadu did Kubla Khan . . .': the poem, Derrida tells you, 'can attach itself to any word at all' (237). For example, 'Xanadu', or 'you'.

THE GIFT

In its cryptically disjunctive, elliptical fashion, 'Che cos'è la poesia?' engages with the ostensibly quite traditional conception of the poem as gift. Coleridge concludes his 1816 preface to 'the Fragment of "Kubla Khan"' by remarking that 'the author has frequently purposed to finish for himself what had been originally, as it were, given to him' (Wu 1998, 522). *Kubla Khan* is or was, apparently, a gift. What is a gift? At various points throughout this study I have been shooting myself in the foot (though I have also at least tried to explain my reasons for doing this) by making generalizations about 'Derrida's work', 'all of Derrida's work', 'Derrida's work in general', and so on. I am now going to do so once again: all of Derrida's work can be approached and thought about starting from the notion of the gift. (For 'gift' in that last sentence you might readily think to substitute 'deconstruction', 'text', 'supplement', 'differance', 'the secret' and so on.) We may suppose that we know what a gift is, and what is happening when we give someone a present or someone gives us a present. It might be a pair of socks or a bunch of flowers. It usually comes in an appropriate package, like nice wrapping paper, with a card. Derrida calls all this into question. He poisons the waters of all 'received ideas' on this topic. ('Gift', as he points out, means 'poison' in German, and also relates back to the *pharmakon* as undecidably 'charm', 'remedy' and 'poison': see GT 12, 36, 54, 69; PP 131–2.) Derrida wonders, interminably, whether there is such a thing as a gift: when speaking of the gift, indeed, he often adds the phrase 'if there is such a thing' or 'if there is any' (see e.g. VR 18–19).

This is one of the places in Derrida's work where the insights of psychoanalysis are perhaps especially crucial. His account seeks to acknowledge the insidious extent to which narcissistic self-gratification or unconscious gratification may be at work in the act of giving. The

in 1820, a poem that is about a bunch of flowers rather than about a pair of socks, or more precisely perhaps it is about the dream of a ghostly nosegay, the desire to gather and present a bunch of flowers, the poem *as* a bunch of flowers. The speaker of the poem recounts a dream in which he 'wander[s] by the way', 'led . . . astray' by the 'gentle odours' of flowers. He provides a sort of micro-anthology ('anthology' is literally a gathering of flowers, from the ancient Greek *anthos*, 'flower', *logia*-, 'gathering') of the flowers he finds ('pied wind-flowers and violets', 'daisies', 'oxslips', 'bluebells', 'lush eglantine' and so on).

Shelley concludes the poem with a stanza that returns him (or the speaker), and us as readers, to the question of the title (*The Question*):

> Methought that of these visionary flowers
> I made a nosegay, bound in such a way
> That the same hues, which in their natural bowers
> Were mingled or opposed, the like array
> Kept these imprisoned children of the Hours
> Within my hand, – and then, elate and gay,
> I hastened to the spot whence I had come,
> That I might there present it! – Oh! to whom?
> (Shelley 1970, 614–15)

If, as its title prompts us to suppose, the poem is not only about a nosegay but also *is* the nosegay it describes, it is a question of the poem itself as gift. The question with which the poem ends ('Oh! to whom?') invokes the experience of the impossibility of the gift as an experience of writing but also of reading. In this scene the reader is spectralized as much as the poet or speaker: the entire 'dream' of the poem is impelled by the desire to 'present it', by the desire that the nosegay and the poem be a gift, but the question remains: 'Oh! to whom?' Hastening beyond but also before any and every reader, the question (and the poem it entitles) is still to be read, still to be presented. The dream of the poem survives, outliving both the poet and every specific, nominal addressee (such as you or me). 'The Question' remains a testimony, in a dream, to the ghostliness of the present: a poem can no more be a gift, perhaps, than can a dream. But for just this reason the poem and the dream become privileged figures for trying to think about the gift. What else is the desire to give if not a desire *in the gift of* a poem or dream, or more precisely and abyssally (in the case of Shelley's *The Question* and

Coleridge's *Kubla Khan*) the dream *of* a poem, a poem *in* a dream, the vision of a poem in a dream?

Just as the 'I' in Shelley's poem perhaps never arrives (back) at 'the spot whence I had come', so the 'I' in *Kubla Khan* is preoccupied with a sort of loop or chiasmus, a looping desire ('Could I revive within me . . .') that in some sense never closes up. In both cases the narrative breaks off, and indeed breaks up its own apparent beginning. Both poems are concerned with the sense of a story or account that must but cannot be narrated. This double bind comports with the notion of the gift as Derrida elaborates it. As he puts it in *Given Time*: 'The gift, if there is any, requires and at the same time excludes the possibility of narrative. The gift is on condition of the narrative, but simultaneously on the condition of possibility and impossibility of the narrative' (GT 103). There cannot be a story about the gift, if there is to have been a gift; but at the same time there *has to be* some story, whether it is in the form of a poem or a preface, about *the impossibility* of the gift: 'That I might there present it! – Oh! to whom?'

What Derrida has said or written about the gift provides another way of thinking about deconstruction, differance, the poematic, and so on. The gift is beyond reason. As Derrida puts it in *Given Time*: 'There is no reason for there ever to be the least gift' (GT 77). The gift is a kind of madness (see GT 35, 58). It has a 'mad energy' (G 243). There must be something 'incalculable' about a gift; it must have the status of 'incalculable or unforeseeable *exception*' (GT 129). The gift is linked with the logic of exorbitance, founding excess or hyperbole that we have encountered elsewhere in this study (for example, in the context of the supplement and the promise). The gift, Derrida declares, 'is *excessive in advance*, a priori *exaggerated*. A donating experience that would not be delivered over, a priori, to some immoderation, in other words, a moderate, measured gift would not be a gift' (GT 38). As with the 'event' of deconstruction, there can be no gift, Derrida suggests, without uncertainty about the distinction between 'the natural and the artificial, the authentic and the inauthentic, the originary and the derived or borrowed' (GT 70). Here we might recall, once again, Coleridge's wording of the 'origin' of the 'gift' called *Kubla Khan*: the poem is something that 'had been originally, as it were, given to him'. The crucially uncertain 'as it were' (about which an entire further chapter might be written) hangs strangely and interminably *between* the 'originally' and the 'given', as well as *over* the notion of the poem as gift.

The gift then, in Derrida's account, is in some respects more irrup-tive, more disruptive than Coleridge's phrasing might suggest. The gift has no essence; it is 'beyond being' (SN 85). It is not a matter of some-thing that can ever be 'given to' *someone* ('originally, as it were, given to him'), any more than it can be given *by* someone. The gift is 'that which one does not have' (SM 27). As soon as we construe the gift in terms of subjects and objects ('Look, here is a gift, I hereby give it to you'), the thinking of the gift is already locked into a logic of give-and-take, circularity and exchange, conscious or unconscious reward or gratification. The gift is mad. It is a madness. Like 'differance', Michael Naas has suggested, 'gift' is the name of 'that which has nothing proper; it is a reference that can have no referent' (Naas 1996, 83). The 'giving of the gift', as Derrida remarks in *Glas*, has to be understood 'before all subjectivity and objectivity' (G 243). It corresponds with what I have been calling a 'poetry break', with the poem or poematic as Derrida traces it in 'Che cos'è la poesia?'. 'The gift of the poem', he suggests, involves the experience of something that 'has no title', that cannot be signed (either by poet or reader), and that 'comes along without your expecting it, cutting short the breath, breaking all ties with discursive and especially literary poetry' (Che 235, tr. mod.). The gift of the poem breaks with every presence, with every question in the form 'what is . . .?' ('what is a poem?', 'what is a gift?') (see Che 237).

12

AFTER DERRIDA

Now, in this final chapter, I am to provide you with some sort of 'after-word'. As the *Routledge Critical Thinkers* editor explains in his Preface: 'Each book [in this series] concludes with a survey of the thinker's impact, outlining how their ideas have been taken up and developed by others' (p. ix). It is a *Routledge Critical Thinkers* convention for this conclusion to come under the form of the heading 'After . . .': 'After Derrida'. After Derrida? I began with a sort of preface entitled 'Why Derrida?', and I tried to answer that question, in other words to treat it in the most serious fash-ion, while also explaining why it seemed to me comical and ridiculous. Derrida's work is of interest precisely to the extent that it questions and transforms the ways in which we might think about the structure and pre-suppositions of a series of books called *Routledge Critical Thinkers*. His thinking is fundamentally incompatible with the project of a text (such as this one was supposed to have been) that sums up the author's work, beginning with a neatly packaged explanation of why this work might be worth reading and ending with a likewise neatly packaged survey of what it was all about and what impact it has had on other thinkers.

    This introduction to Derrida has tried to communicate a sense of his work as uncanny. Derrida's work renders all our familiar notions, struc-tures and presuppositions strange. We may suppose we know what a book is, what a summary or survey is, or a preface, or an afterword, or where a book begins and ends: Derrida offers no such assurances. As he puts it in *Of Grammatology*: 'The idea of the book, which always refers to a natural totality, is profoundly alien to the sense of writing' (OG 18). As I have tried to demonstrate, Derrida's notion of writing – linked to his notions of trace, remainder, supplement, differance and text – radically alters the bases on which we might think about thinking, consciousness, presence, being, humanity, animality, divinity, identity, intention, decision, responsibility, justice, friendship, desire, memory, death and language, as well as about so many discourses or practices.

Derrida's work continues to have a profound impact across the entire terrain: as I suggested early on in this study, its impact comprises an earthquake or, rather, an unending series of earthquakes. What follows, perforce, is not so much a summary as an attempt to trace a few faults, cracks or fissures in or around the idea of a chapter called 'After Derrida'.

In what might operate as a kind of preliminary sortie, permit me to suggest just a few of the areas in (or between) which you might wish to consider the impact or impacts of Derrida's work. (Parenthetical references here are to material listed in the 'Works on and around Jacques Derrida' in the 'Further reading' section at the end of this chapter, see pp. 163–71.) Tremors and upheavals can be witnessed in and around literary studies (see Clark 1992; Culler 1983; Hillis Miller, 'Derrida and Literature', in Cohen 2001); philosophy (Gasché 1986; Bennington 1993; 'Deconstruction and the Philosophers' in Bennington 1994); psychoanalysis (Ellmann in Royle 2000; 'Circanalysis' in Bennington 2000); politics (Beardsworth 1996; Lacoue-Labarthe and Nancy 1997; Sprinker 1999; Bennington in Cohen 2001); history (Attridge, Bennington and Young 1987; Fenves in Cohen 2001); religion (Caputo 1997; de Vries 1999); science (Johnson 1993, 1998; Plotnitsky 1994; Norris 1997); ethics (Critchley 1999; Bennington in Royle 2000); legal studies (Cardozo 1990, 1991); technology (Clark in Royle 2000; Stiegler in Cohen 2001); feminism and sexual difference (Elam 1993; Holland 1997; Feder *et al.* 1997; Kamuf in Cohen 2001); cultural studies (Spivak in Royle 2000, Hall 2002); architecture (Papadakis, Cooke and Benjamin 1989; Wigley 1993); the university (Rand 1992; Readings 1996; Kamuf 1997); theories of education (Biesta and Egéa-Kuehne 2001); 'post theory' (McQuillan *et al.* 1999); postcolonialism (Bhabha 1994; Rooney 2000; Young in Royle 2000); speech act theory (Butler 1997; Hillis Miller 2002); writing fiction (Cixous 1993); inspiration (Clark 1997); and monstrosity ('Monstrism' 2002).

There are problems with the brief (but I hope helpful) list of references, authorial names and dates that I have just evoked. In particular it might convey the impression that Derrida's work (or 'deconstruction') is something that belongs to such and such a time, that it has a measurable impact (registering on some sort of fantasy Critical Thinkers Richter scale), that it has a straightforward afterwards, and correspondingly that it can have a straightforward afterword. Can deconstruction have an afterword? In a short text entitled 'Afterw.rds' Derrida responds that 'it *can't*, but it *must*' (Aft 198–9). This response is characteristic of deconstruction in demanding that we try to engage with the thinking of a double bind, in particular as the experience of what is impossible ('it *can't*') but necessary ('it *must*'), necessary *and* impossible. Deconstruction, he argues, ' "lives" on this "contradiction"', according to which 'the necessary is impossible, or rather the impossible necessary' (Aft 200). Deconstruction *can't* have an afterword, Derrida explains,

> in so far as the hypothesis of an afterword to deconstruction assumes that the discourse of deconstruction has the form of a concluded, closed, closed-off totality, a book, the great Book after which and outside which a postface or a postscript would add a second 'last word', a second term.
>
> (Aft 199)

Deconstruction, as I have tried to make clear in this book, has to do with the supplementary. And it is for this reason that 'deconstruction *must* have the afterword it cannot have'. Derrida goes on to explain:

> For, always incomplete, of an incompletion which is not the negativity of a lack, [deconstruction] is interminable, an 'interminable analysis' ('theoretical and practical', as we used to say [see, for example, Pos 90]). As it is never closed into a system, as it is the deconstruction of the systemic totality, it needs some supplementary afterword each time it runs the risk of stabilizing or saturating into a formalized discourse (doctrine, method, delimitable and canonized corpus, teachable knowledge, etc.) . . . [Deconstruction would be] *afterword to the presence or presentation of the present itself*.
>
> (Aft 199)

After Derrida. I could imagine someone writing a book about this phrase. Perhaps me? As has been remarked, 'after' in this context has at least three meanings: (1) 'after' in a temporal sense (as in 'later than', 'in the wake of'); (2) 'after' in the sense of 'following in search of' (as in, 'I'm after Derrida. Has anyone seen him?'); (3) 'after' in the sense of 'in honour of', 'according to', 'in agreement with' or 'in the manner of' (as in 'after Rembrandt'). (See Royle 1995, 2–5.) The phrase 'After Derrida' is already divided in its sense of the present, leaving us uncertain about whether it is a question of the past or of the future, or of the past *as* future. Indeed each of these three senses of 'after' is fractured, fissured, opened up to being thought anew and differently *after Derrida*. Take sense (3), for example. In truth Derrida never writes simply 'according to' or 'in agreement with', let alone 'in the manner of'. His work is guided by the logic of the supplement, by the fact that a writer can always say 'more, less, or something other than what he [or she] *would mean*' (OG 158). Even when he writes explicitly 'in honour of' another thinker or writer, Derrida always supplements and alters, interrupts and interferes with our sense of the so-called original. His characteristic double gesture of respect and disrespect, or of betraying through fidelity, is fundamentally at odds with any merely imitative or reduplicative reading or writing. The last thing Derrida's work seems to call for is a sort of parroting or regurgitation of his 'ideas', 'style', etc. Rather it affirms singularity, the implacable 'desire for idiom', and does so differently in every text.

For thinking about how to read or how to write after Derrida, this is at once challenging and exhilarating. No other contemporary 'critical thinker' has perhaps been more scrupulous in questioning the nature of mastery, and in arguing that 'the master is nothing' (MO 23) and that 'mastery . . . is never itself' (AFRC 78). No doubt there remains the irony of Derrida as a grandmaster of non-mastery. Perhaps an especially helpful way of exploring this irony would be in reckoning with the singularity of his work as an affirmation of non-belonging. As he puts it, with deceptive simplicity, in an interview: 'do not consider me "one of you", "don't count me in"' (TS 27). Derrida is not 'one of the family', as he says: 'I do not identify myself with a linguistic community, a national community, a political party, or with any group or clique whatsoever, with any philosophical or literary school' (27). Being 'not one of the family' means, among other things, being not one of the group called 'grandmasters'. But 'don't count me in' also means 'don't count yourself in': be free, experience the impossible, 'everything remains open, still to be thought' (U 131).

Derrida can crack you up. As I have tried to suggest in the preceding pages, his work is very serious but it also seeks constantly to keep itself open to a certain laughter, play and irony. It questions any discourse that, like the speech act theorist John Searle's, 'seriously suppos[es] itself to know all about the difference between the serious and the non-serious' (LI 35). This does not mean that his reading of Searle is not also, at the same time, 'exceedingly serious' (65). Correspondingly, Derrida takes the work of Heidegger very seriously (a good deal more seriously than do many other contemporary philosophers and 'critical thinkers'). But in characterizing Heidegger as a philosopher in whose work 'there is little room for laughter' (PF 57), Derrida's work might be taken as offering at once a *less and more* serious legacy. This legacy is not simple: the phrase 'after Derrida' is, after all, an interminable evocation of the question of legacy. But it is a legacy haunted by 'a certain laughter' (see Diff 27; and for 'differance' in particular as a question of legacy, see AIIWP 366). This is the sort of laughter that Derrida talks about or tries to listen to in James Joyce's *Ulysses* (in UG). It is a laughter that *'remains'*, Derrida stresses, a laughter of affirmation, a 'yes-laughter' the analysis of which 'is not exhausted by any of the available forms of knowledge' (UG 294–5). It would perhaps be apt, then, to remark here on a sense of laughter around the phrase 'after Derrida'. As the essay on Joyce may suggest, Derrida's work can be very funny, and this sense of humour is inescapably part of his legacy. It is a funniness that comes perhaps always already with a hint of the funny-strange or funny-uncanny: we might recall here, for example, that his devastating, at moments hilarious account of Searle in *Limited Inc* starts off by remarking on a sense of 'strange, uncanny familiarity' (LI 29) in response to Searle's work.

Derrida makes a joke in a footnote to one of the short texts (WIP) published in *Points . . . Interviews 1974–94*. He is talking about a collection of essays edited by Richard Wolin that included a poor and unauthorized translation of one of Derrida's texts together with a quite ill-informed and irresponsible commentary by Wolin on the subject of Derrida's work. Derrida complained about this unauthorized translation. A revised edition of Wolin's book appeared, without Derrida's text in it. In an advertisement the new publisher (MIT Press) drew attention to 'the absence from this edition of an interview with Jacques Derrida'. In the footnote in *Points . . .* Derrida remarks:

> The most novel thing [about this revised edition of Wolin's book] seems to me
> to be in the nature of the publicity. The publisher ... advertised the book
> commercially by using once again my name in order, in effect, to recommend
> to potential buyers a book whose only interest lay, if one were to believe the
> advertisement, in the fact that a text by Derrida was missing from it!! Has
> anyone ever seen such a thing? I don't think so. The strength and the interest
> of a book, even its commercialization, would here reside in the very 'absence'
> of the text that is not included in it. What dissemination! What power of
> absence! ... All at once I started to daydream. ... [W]hat if now this practice
> of advertising academic books were to spread ... [i]f all of a sudden people
> started citing my name in order to recommend all the books that include no text
> of mine? 'Buy this book, even read it, it doesn't have any text by Derrida!' Just
> imagine the career I could have!
>
> (WIP 485)

MIT's advertising strategy provokingly illustrates just how well-known the name 'Derrida' has become. Derrida's daydream might be my nightmare: here in this concluding chapter I am supposed to offer an account not only of the literally thousands of books in which Derrida's work is discussed – in which his ideas are 'taken up and developed by others' – but also of all the other books, of all the literally millions of books in which 'Derrida' is (apparently) absent.

I began this book with a 'first' quote from Derrida: 'Be alert to these invisible quotation marks, even within a word' (LO 76). As I have suggested, being alert to invisible quotation marks, to the point of 'destabiliz[ing] . . . the opposition between discourse *with* and discourse *without* quotation marks' (SST 75), would be one way of describing what his work is about. As his anecdotal daydream already intimates, there should perhaps be quotation marks around the word 'absent', for example. 'Absent' might be felt to merit what Derrida has called the 'small clothespins' (SST 77) of quote marks because, after Derrida, it is no longer possible to assume that we know what we mean when we say that the 'thought' or 'impact' of a particular author is present or absent in a particular text. Differance, let us recall, is 'neither a presence nor an absence. No ontology can think its operation' (OG 314). If Derrida's 'final intention' in *Of Grammatology*, is 'to render enigmatic what one thinks one understands' by the word 'presence' (OG 70), it is also a matter of seeing how 'absence' is made strange.

As I have tried to make clear in the preceding pages, the logic of the supplement or differance (or the trace, etc.) entails a kind of 'thought without meaning' (see OG 93). It entails effects that do not belong, effects that neither simply originate in nor return to a particular thinker. At the same time, however, Derrida's work leads us to a new sense of the importance of singularity, of trying to respect the singularity of a given text or thinker: his readings have a way of bringing out new, sometimes very strange 'presences' in this text or thinker. After Derrida, texts come to say things their authors might never have imagined (even 'unconsciously': Derrida is not Freud; deconstruction is not psychoanalysis). After Derrida, one has to reckon with 'presences' that are neither simply inside nor categorically outside the text. After Derrida, texts are haunted in a newly legible fashion: 'the text is no longer the snug airtight inside of an interiority or an identity-to-itself' (O 36). Along with innumerable other oppositions or alleged opposites (same and other, life and death, speech and writing, literature and philosophy, respect and betrayal, and so on), the relations between inside and outside, text and world, are strangely changed.

—————— The impact of Derrida's work might least badly be summed up as a spectralization, as something that goes bump in the day as much as night. His work prompts new ways of thinking about presences and absences, the haunting of one by the other. His work has ghostly impact. (This has led, among other things, to an increasing interest in the relationship between Derrida's work and 'the Gothic': see, for example, Castricano 2001 and Wolfreys 2002.) It is in some respects the bump or impact of something eerily weightless: differance 'has no weight' (OG 93), as he has noted. This spooky impact has been so immense that people really do advertise and even write books drawing attention to Derrida's absence from them. We could consider, for example, Hillel Schwartz's 560-page book *The Culture of the Copy: Striking Likenesses, Unreasonable Facsimiles* which includes as an entry in the pages of its index: 'Derrida, Jacques, nary an appearance in the text' (Schwartz 1996, 543). What is happening when someone feels impelled to remark upon the 'absence' of Derrida in this fashion? How should we analyse Derrida's 'impact' in such a context?

Take, for example, Derrida's work in relation to film studies. Antony Easthope begins an essay on 'Derrida and British Film Theory' with an epigraph from Rob Lapsley and Michael Westlake: 'Within film theory Derrida is perhaps best conceived of as a structuring absence' (see Easthope 1996, 184). Easthope goes on to examine the importance of the British film journal *Screen* in the 1970s, in particular its dominant and explicit concerns with the Marxism of Louis Althusser and the psychoanalytic 'lessons' of Jacques Lacan. He argues that writers involved with *Screen*, such as Colin MacCabe and Stephen Heath, were evidently aware of Derrida's work, but did not explicitly engage with it. This then enables Easthope to clarify the force of his opening epigraph: 'Like off-screen space, the writing of Derrida performs as a structuring absence in the work of *Screen*' (Easthope 189). Easthope's conclusion corroborates other accounts, such as Brunette and Wills (1989), Byrne and McQuillan (1999) and Smith (2000), in proposing a seismic shift and new alignments in thinking about 'Derrida and film'.

━━━━━━ Elsewhere, especially in literature and philosophy, Derrida's 'presence' may for many years have seemed quite obvious. For many, Derrida's work has changed the ways in which we are obliged to approach that 'strange institution called literature' (TSICL) as well as the putatively normal institution called philosophy. But Derrida's remains in many ways a ghostly presence, even when it is apparently most palpable. In some cases his work leaves its mark by apparently *not* doing so. Hillel Schwartz's evidently proud but also anxious index reference bears witness to this. On a larger scale we could say that what is called 'analytical philosophy' or 'Anglo-Saxon philosophy' continues mostly to disavow the existence of Derrida's work, to act or make-believe it is not there. (A useful counter-example here would be a recent collection of essays entitled *Arguing with Derrida*: see Glendinning 2001.) And in a still more general context, it is necessary to consider the ways in which a thinker can have a profound impact on people who have never read his or her work, or indeed have never heard of the thinker in question. Paul de Man makes this point when he remarks on the 'impact' of Hegel: 'Whether we know it, or like it, or not, most of us are Hegelians and quite orthodox ones at that. . . . Few thinkers have so many disciples who never read a word of their master's writings' (de Man 1996, 92–3). Even if we have never read Derrida, we live, as I suggested at the beginning, in a Derridean epoch.

It seems clear that this phrase 'After Derrida' is about death, the death of Jacques Derrida but also, for example, your death or mine. Such is the death-driven structure of a volume in the *Routledge Critical Thinkers* series: we start with a chapter entitled 'Why X?' (Why should the existence of this 'thinker' be of any interest to us? Couldn't we get along perfectly well without him or her?), and we end with a chapter entitled 'After X'. 'After Derrida': that's him then, dead and buried, done and dusted, at last we have finished with him and can get on with the rest of our lives. He may not actually be dead yet, but it is difficult not to feel that he is, or *ought to be*, as far as the *Routledge Critical Thinkers* series is concerned. Here, once again, we should perhaps try to read and listen to what Derrida himself has to say, for example in an essay on *Hamlet*: 'one must stop believing that the dead are just the departed and that the departed do nothing. One must stop pretending to know what is meant by "to die" and especially by "dying". One has, then, to talk about spectrality' (TOJ 30).

The phrase 'after Derrida' evokes, then, the question of mourning. Until now I have used the phrase 'Derrida's work' without specifically emphasizing that, for him, all 'work', every work is a 'work of mourning' (see, for example, SM 97). As he summarizes what is perhaps the essential concern of *Glas*: 'mourning-work is not just any kind of work but something like the "essence" of work' (Ja 52). All of his writing is in some sense 'bereaved' or in at least 'semi-' or 'demi-mourning' (Dia 143). Mourning is in the name: as we have seen, the name carries death. 'Derrida' requires no 'after' in order to be a name-inscribed-by-death. The prefix 'after' is in this respect just a sort of further twist of the knife, the 'after' as afterthought. In a sense everyone who bears a proper name is living 'after' themselves, thanks to the deadly power of their name. This is not something to feel miserable about, in Derrida's view. At issue here, among other things, is a notion of desire to be distinguished from that of Lacan and other psychoanalytical accounts. Desire, for Derrida, is not about 'loss' and 'lack' but about 'affirmation'. Thus he declares: 'I believe desire is affirmation, and consequently that mourning itself is affirmation' (Dia 143).

We only ever love what is mortal and the mortality of what we love is not something accidental and exterior, but rather is the condition of love. Derrida sees fissures in the psychoanalytic conception of mourning, in particular in Freud's apparently rigid notion of 'normal' mourning. For Freud, there is normal mourning and this is something that comes to an end. The work of mourning is teleological. As he puts it, in the essay 'Mourning and Melancholia' (1917): 'The fact is . . . that when the work of mourning is completed the ego becomes free and uninhibited again' (Freud 1984, 253). The death, loss or disappearance of something or someone beloved is something painful but fundamentally accidental. For Derrida, too, it is of course painful (and the funeral speeches and related writings published as *The Work of Mourning* [WoM] movingly and hauntingly attest to this), but it is also a necessary possibility that structures the very movement of identification, of being an 'I', of loving oneself or another.

As he has said in various contexts (indeed in a sense this is what he says all the time, in everything he writes): 'I always love what I have loved' (see, for example, U 122, Dia 152). Love, for Derrida, is till death us do part, or rather it is on condition that we are in some sense *always already parted* both from one another *and* from ourselves: 'I mourn therefore I am' (Ist 321) would be Derrida's rewriting of the Cartesian 'I think therefore I am'. The 'I am' is possible only on the basis of memory, language and others. My relation to myself is, from before the word go (or the word 'gaga' or 'mamma' or 'me'), 'plunged into mourning' (Ist 321). Or as he aphoristically encapsulates it in an essay on the psychoanalytic writings of Nicolas Abraham and Maria Torok: 'The Self: a cemetery guard' (F xxxv).

For Derrida there is no such thing as normal mourning, unless we grant that the normal is the impossible. The concept of mourning entails a logic of double-bind, an aporia whereby 'success fails' and 'failure succeeds' (M 35). One has to keep the memory of the loved one within oneself, to remain faithful in memory and to the memory of the beloved. At the same time, one has to let the other remain other, in other words to ensure that the other is not assimilated or effectively wiped out as other. A refusal to mourn (which in a conventional psychoanalytic description is identified with 'abnormal' mourning) is thus for Derrida an inseparable part of mourning. Mourning is necessarily divided, semi, demi, double mourning. If, as I hope to have shown in the course of this book, Derrida is a great thinker of fidelity, this is fidelity in mourning. As he remarks:

> the faithful one is someone who is in mourning. Mourning is an interiorization of the dead other, but it is also the contrary. Hence the impossibility of

completing one's mourning and even the will not to mourn are also forms of fidelity. If to mourn and not to mourn are two forms of fidelity and two forms of infidelity, the only thing remaining – and this is where I speak of semi-mourning – is an experience between the two. I cannot complete my mourning for everything I lose, because I want to keep it, and at the same time, what I do best is to mourn, is to lose it, because by mourning, I keep it inside me.

(Dia 151–2)

At stake in all of this is another thinking of 'the political', where 'politics' is figured as first and foremost 'an organization of the time and space of mourning' (A 61). (For more on Derrida and mourning, see, in particular, Krell 2000.)

After Derrida? It's war. As I have tried to make clear, Derrida's writing is war writing. His work is, in the strongest sense of the word, *polemical* (from the ancient Greek 'polemos', meaning 'war'). He is acutely sensitive to questions of language as constituting the basis and medium of all sorts of dispute, conflict and violence. As he puts it in 'Force of Law': 'A sort of *polemos* already concerns the appropriation of language' (FL 923). If 'language gives rise only to appropriative madness, to jealousy without appropriation', as he suggests in *Monolingualism of the Other*, this is because 'there is no natural property of language' (MO 24). Elsewhere he declares: 'There is a war raging for and by means of the property of language, among philosophers and between them and others' (LMT 178). 'Language' here refers both to a so-called national language and to the notion of having a language of one's own (starting, perhaps, with one's own so-called proper name). In essays on topics varying from literature (in TWJ) to 'today's Europe' (in OH), Derrida has shown a consistent concern with the insidious power of what he calls 'the Anglo-American language' (OH 23), with the stakes of 'a *war* through which English tries to erase the other language or languages, to colonize them, to domesticate them' (TWJ 156). This book, written in English, will also have been, in its own manner, at war *with* English. In these pages I have sought, in however limited a fashion, to open up some of the possibilities of thinking about the English language *after Derrida*.

Since at least the mid-1960s Derrida has been concerned with what he terms 'the effective violence of disseminating writing' (Pos 85), with deconstruction as 'a strategy without finality' (Diff 7), with the economy of differance as a 'war economy' (O 5). 'Deconstruction', he insists, 'is not *neutral*. It *intervenes*' (Pos 93). Whether he is arguing for the value of the non-serious, for the impossibility of 'true mourning' (M 35) or for the haunting and ineffaceable effects of the undecidable, Derrida's work is at war. As he remarks in *Mémoires*: 'in the war that rages over the subject of deconstruction, there is no front: there are no fronts' (M 18).

All of which is not to suggest that the writings of Jacques Derrida should be regarded as simply belligerent. On the contrary, after Derrida, we need to rethink the very terms of battle, the very nature of war – whether a war between nation-states or between lovers, a war against terrorism or oneself. 'A new discourse on war is necessary' (PS 246), as he argues in a recent essay on psychoanalysis. Derrida doubts that 'violence is an evil' and conceives his texts as working against the 'bad violence' of 'brutality' (TS 90–2). Yet his preoccupation with the figure of the earthquake, in interviews and elsewhere, is evidently inflected by the sense that, in itself, 'an earthquake is not violent', since 'there is no natural violence' (TS 92). His concern with differance is with a sort of 'nonviolence' that in its very 'weakness' or weightlessness is 'terrible' (ATED 137). Differance, as he writes in 'Psyche: Inventions of the Other', is 'without status, without law, without a horizon of reappropriation, programmation, institutional legitimation'. The last words here cannot, must not be the last word. On the contrary, like the 'come' discussed earlier in this book, they would open onto the future itself, after Derrida:

> Differance . . . remains very gentle, foreign to threats and wars. But for that it is felt as something all the more dangerous.
>
> Like the future. For the time to come is its only concern: allowing the adventure or the event of the entirely other to come. Of an entirely other that can no longer be confused with the God or the Man of ontotheology or with any of the figures of the configuration (the subject, consciousness, the unconscious, the self, man or woman, and so on).
>
> (PIO 61)

FURTHER READING

WORKS BY JACQUES DERRIDA

As I have tried to suggest in the preceding pages, Derrida is a great talker as well as a great writer. Coming to his work for the first time, you may find it most helpful to combine reading some of his interviews with reading some of the more important essays or other short texts. I have divided up this section of the bibliography into 'Interviews and Other Discussions with Derrida', 'Top Ten Essays and Other Short Texts by Derrida', 'Derrida Anthologies' and 'A Chronology of Selected Books by Derrida'. I would emphasize that this bibliography makes no attempt at being exhaustive (though it may make exhausting reading!). More detailed bibliographical information on works by or about Derrida can be found in, for example: William B. Schultz and Lewis L.B. Fried, *Jacques Derrida: An Annotated Primary and Secondary Bibliography* (Garland, 1992); Albert Leventure, 'A Jacques Derrida Bibliography 1962–90', in *Textual Practice*, 5: 1 (1991); Geoffrey Bennington, 'Bibliography', in Bennington and Derrida, *Jacques Derrida* (Chicago: Chicago University Press, 1993); Martin McQuillan, 'Bibliography', in *Deconstruction: A Reader* (Edinburgh: Edinburgh University Press, 2000); and, most up-to-date, Peter Krapp's Bibliography on the internet, at www.hydra. umn.edu/derrida.

INTERVIEWS AND OTHER DISCUSSIONS WITH DERRIDA

Positions, trans. Alan Bass (Chicago: Chicago University Press, 1981). (An invaluable series of interviews dating from 1967, 1968 and 1971. Especially helpful for an understanding of the early impact of deconstruction and the politics of Derrida's work.)

Roundtable Discussions (1979) in *The Ear of the Other: Otobiography, Transference, Translation*, trans. Peggy Kamuf, ed. Christie V. McDonald (New York: Schocken Books, 1985). (Includes illuminating discussions of a range of topics including the name, the signature, translation and psychoanalysis.)

'Deconstruction and the Other' (1981), interview with Richard Kearney, in Kearney's *Dialogues with Contemporary Continental Thinkers* (Manchester: Manchester University Press, 1984), 105–26. (An especially accessible text for an understanding of 'otherness' in Derrida's work.)

'Deconstruction in America: An Interview with Jacques Derrida', trans. James Creech, *Critical Exchange*, 17 (1985): 1–33. (Interesting for the discussion of deconstruction not only in relation to literary studies but also in relation to theology and religion, particularly in the US.)

Points . . . Interviews, 1974–94, ed. Elisabeth Weber, trans. Peggy Kamuf and others (Stanford: Stanford University Press, 1995). (The most wide-ranging and indispensable collection of interviews currently available.)

'This Strange Institution Called Literature' (1989), trans. Geoffrey Bennington and Rachel Bowlby, in *Acts of Literature*, ed. Derek Attridge (London and New York: Routledge, 1992), 33–75. (One of the most clarifying interviews especially on notions of literature and singularity.)

'The Deconstruction of Actuality: An Interview with Jacques Derrida' (1993), trans. Jonathan Rée, in *Deconstruction: A Reader* ed. Martin McQuillan, (Edinburgh: Edinburgh University Press, 2000), 527–53. (Also published in N and TE.) (A very helpful interview in terms of the discussion of politics, spectrality, messianicity and teletechnology.)

'The Villanova Roundtable: A Conversation with Jacques Derrida' (1994), in *Deconstruction in a Nutshell*, ed. John D. Caputo (New York: Fordham University Press, 1997), 3–28. (Particularly helpful on deconstruction, religion, justice and the gift.)

'I Have a Taste for the Secret', Jacques Derrida in conversation with Maurizio Ferraris and Giorgio Vattimo, in Derrida and Ferraris, *A Taste for the Secret*, trans. Giacomo Donis (Cambridge, England: Polity, 2001), pp. 3–92. (Conversations taking place in 1993–5, offering an excellent, relatively informal account of many of Derrida's 'key ideas'.)

Perhaps or Maybe, Philosophical Forum (8 March 1996): Jacques Derrida with Alexander García Düttmann. Cassette recording available from the Institute of Contemporary Arts, London. Also published in *Responsibilities of Deconstruction*, eds Jonathon Dronsfield and Nick Midgley, *PLI*, Warwick Journal of Philosophy, vol. 6 (University of Warwick, 1997): 1–18.

D'ailleurs Derrida (Derrida Elsewhere). A film by Safaa Fathy. Gloria Films, 1999. (Mostly in French, with English subtitles, shot in various locations including Algeria, Spain, the US, and 'at home' in Paris, this beautiful film communicates a fine sense of Derrida 'in person', talking about such assorted topics as music, fish, time, religion, secrets and his library.)

Negotiations: Interventions and Interviews, 1971–2001, ed. and trans. Elizabeth Rottenberg (Stanford: Stanford University Press, 2002). (As its subtitle makes clear, not only interviews but also short 'occasional' pieces, letters, transcriptions of improvised interventions at press conferences, and so on. An excellent collection, especially for thinking about issues of ethics, politics and science in relation to Derrida's work.)

TOP TEN: ESSAYS AND OTHER SHORT TEXTS BY DERRIDA

I list below just ten short texts that I would consider especially accessible and/or important for an initial engagement with Derrida's work. The date of first publication or of original delivery as a lecture is given in brackets.

'Structure, Sign, and Play in the Discourse of the Human Sciences' (1966), in *Writing and Difference*, trans. Alan Bass (London: Routledge and Kegan Paul, 1978), 278–93.

'". . . That Dangerous Supplement . . ."' (1967), in *Of Grammatology*, trans. Gayatri Chakravorty Spivak (Baltimore: Johns Hopkins University Press, 1976), 141–64. (Also published in Derek Attridge's anthology, AL.)

'Différance' (1968), in *Margins of Philosophy*, trans. Alan Bass (Chicago: Chicago University Press, 1982), 1–27. (Extracts also published in Peggy Kamuf's anthology, DRBB.)

'Plato's Pharmacy' (1968), in *Dissemination*, trans. Barbara Johnson (Chicago: Chicago University Press, 1981), 63–171. (Extracts also published in Peggy Kamuf's anthology, DRBB.)

'Signature Event Context' (1971), trans. Samuel Weber and Jeffrey Mehlman, in *Limited Inc* (Evanston, Illinois: Northwestern University Press, 1988), 1–23. (Also published in Peggy Kamuf's anthology, DRBB.)

'The Time of a Thesis: Punctuations' (1980), in *Philosophy in France Today*, ed. Alan Montefiore (Cambridge: Cambridge University Press, 1983), 34–50. (This is the text of Derrida's thesis-defence in 1980 and provides what is perhaps the most concise and helpful summary of his literary and philosophical concerns from the early 1960s to the end of the 1970s.)

'Before the Law' (1982), trans. Avital Ronell and Christine Roulston, in *Acts of Literature*, ed. Derek Attridge (London and New York: Routledge, 1992), 181–220.

'Letter to a Japanese Friend' (1983), in *Derrida and Differance*, eds. Robert Bernasconi and David Wood (Warwick: Parousia Press, 1985), 1–8. (Also published in Peggy Kamuf's anthology, DRBB.) (A short but very illuminating text in which Derrida talks about the idea of translating the word 'deconstruction' into Japanese and about the relationship between deconstruction and translation.)

'Some Statements and Truisms about Neo-Logisms, Newisms, Postisms, Parasitisms, and Other Small Seismisms' (1987), trans. Anne Tomiche, in *The States of 'Theory': History, Art and Critical Discourse*, ed. David Carroll (New York: Columbia University Press, 1990), 63–95. (Especially helpful on questions of history in relation to Derrida's work.)

'Afterword: Toward an Ethic of Discussion' (1988), trans. Samuel Weber, in *Limited Inc* (Evanston, Illinois: Northwestern University Press, 1988), 111–60. (Looks back to 'Signature Event Context' and its aftermath: see LI for fuller details. 'Afterword' offers very clear and helpful discussion of a number of topics including undecidability, ethics, fiction and 'real life'.)

DERRIDA ANTHOLOGIES

Anidjar, Gil, ed. *Acts of Religion* (London and New York: Routledge, 2002). (A valuable collection of essays demonstrating Derrida's long-standing concerns with issues of religion.)

Attridge, Derek, ed. *Acts of Literature* (London and New York: Routledge, 1992). (An excellent anthology for anyone interested in Derrida's work from a literary point of view. Attridge provides a very helpful introduction as well as headnotes to each of the essays in the volume.)

Kamuf, Peggy, ed. *A Derrida Reader: Between the Blinds* (London and New York: Harvester Wheatsheaf, 1991). (A fine selection of texts. Kamuf also provides an excellent introduction and headnotes to individual pieces.)

McQuillan, Martin, ed. *Deconstruction: A Reader* (Edinburgh: Edinburgh University Press, 2000). (A valuable collection, offering texts by Derrida and other contemporary critical thinkers as well as earlier writers including Marx, Freud, Benjamin and Heidegger.)

Wolfreys, Julian, *The Derrida Reader: Writing Performances* (Edinburgh: Edinburgh University Press, 1998). (A very useful anthology which includes important essays not collected in book-form elsewhere, such as 'Scribble (writing power)', 'The *Retrait* of Metaphor' and 'Econo-mimesis'.)

A CHRONOLOGY OF SELECTED BOOKS BY DERRIDA

Below are listed, in chronological order of first publication in French, some of Derrida's best-known and most influential books. The abbreviation in brackets refers to the English publication: see the 'Abbreviations of Texts by Derrida' section at the beginning of this book.

'act' indeed becomes impossible in Derrida's terms. For whoever gives can only give what he or she cannot perceive, even unconsciously. As he describes it in *Given Time*:

> *At the limit, the gift as gift* ought *not appear as gift: either to the donee or to the donor.* It cannot be gift as gift except by not being present as gift. . . . If the other perceives or receives it, if he or she keeps it as gift, the gift is annulled. But the one who gives it must not see it or know it either; otherwise he begins, at the threshold, as soon as he intends to give, to pay himself with a symbolic recognition, to praise himself, to approve of himself, to gratify himself, to congratulate himself, to give back to himself symbolically the value of what he thinks he has given or what he is preparing to give.

(GT 14)

Another thinking of the 'I' or 'you' is at issue here: there is no donor or donee before the gift, but the gift itself, if there is such a thing, does not belong to any present. As Derrida puts it: '[the] conditions of possibility of the gift (that some "one" gives some "thing" to some "one other") designate simultaneously the conditions of the impossibility of the gift' (GT 12). There is no giving or receiving without the irruptive force of the gift as the impossible (see WB 199), of what cannot be present if there is to be a present. 'The impossibility or double-bind of the gift: For there to be gift, it is necessary that the gift not even appear, that it not be perceived or received as gift' (GT 16).

It is perhaps worth emphasizing that Derrida is not therefore suggesting we stop bothering to think about gifts or that we stop using the vocabulary of 'gift', 'present', 'donation', etc.). On the contrary, he seeks to affirm the gift precisely *in the experience of its impossibility*:

> If the gift is another name of the impossible, we still think it, we name it, we desire it. We intend it. And this *even if* or *because* or *to the extent that* we *never* encounter it, we never know it, we never verify it, we never experience it in its present existence or in its phenomenon. The gift *itself* . . . will never be confused with the presence of its phenomenon.

(GT 29)

Why does one write or want to write a poem? For whom is a poem written? What is a poem? What is the relation between the poem and the gift? We might here briefly consider Shelley's *The Question*, written

1962

L'origine de la géométrie, de Husserl: Introduction et traduction / Edmund Husserl's 'Origin of Geometry': An Introduction (OGI).

1967

L'écriture et la différence / Writing and Difference (WD).
La voix et le phénomène / Speech and Phenomena (SP).
De la grammatologie / Of Grammatology (OG).

1972

La dissémination / Dissemination (D).
Marges — de la philosophie / Margins of Philosophy (MP).
Positions / Positions (Pos).

1973

L'archéologie du frivole / The Archeology of the Frivolous (AFRC).

1974

Glas / Glas (G).

1978

Éperons. Les styles de Nietzsche / Spurs: Nietzsche's Styles (Sp).
La vérité en peinture / The Truth in Painting (TP).

1980

La carte postale, de Socrate à Freud et au-delà / The Post Card: From Socrates to Freud and Beyond (PC).

1983

Signsponge / Signéponge (S).

1987

De l'esprit: Heidegger et la question / Of Spirit: Heidegger and the Question (OS).

1988

Mémoires, Pour Paul de Man / Mémoires: for Paul de Man (M).

1990

Mémoires d'aveugle, L'autoportrait et autres ruines / Memoirs of the Blind: The Self-Portrait and Other Ruins (MB).

Du droit à la philosophie / (the first half published in English as *Who's Afraid of Philosophy*) (WAP).

1991

L'autre cap / The Other Heading (OH).

'Circonfession' in *Jacques Derrida*, Jacques Derrida et Geoffrey Bennington / 'Circumfession' (C).

Donner le temps, 1. La fausse monnaie / Given Time: 1. Counterfeit Money (GT).

1992

Points de suspension / Points . . . (P).

1993

Sauf le nom / 'Sauf le nom' (in ON).

Passions / 'Passions' (in ON).

Khōra / 'Khōra' (in ON).

Spectres de Marx / Specters of Marx (SM).

1994

Politiques de l'amitié / Politics of Friendship (PF).

1995

Mal d'archive / Archive Fever (AF).

1996

Apories / Aporias (A).

Le monolinguisme de l'autre / Monolingualism of the Other (MO).

Résistances − de la psychanalyse / Resistances of Psychoanalysis (RP).

1997

Adieu à Emmanuel Lévinas / Adieu to Emmanuel Levinas (Ad).

De l'hospitalité / Of Hospitality (Hos).

1998

Demeure, Maurice Blanchot (Dem).

1999

Donner la mort (revised edition) / *The Gift of Death* (GD).

'L'animal que donc je suis' (in *L'animal autobiographique: Autour de Jacques Derrida*) (ATA).

2000

Le toucher, Jean-Luc Nancy.

2001

De quoi demain . . . Dialogue (with Elisabeth Roudinesco).

Papier Machine.

2002

Artaud le Moma: Interjections d'appel.

Fichus: Discours de Francfort.

H.C. pour la vie, c'est à dire . . .

2003

Voyous.

WORKS ON AND AROUND JACQUES DERRIDA

Again, the list provided here is necessarily very selective. Below are simply a few of what I consider to be the most helpful and stimulating books specifically concerned with expounding, as well as elaborating on, Derrida's work.

Attridge, Derek, Geoffrey Bennington and Robert Young, eds. *Post-Structuralism and the Question of History*. Cambridge: Cambridge University Press, 1987. (A provoking and important collection of essays on the impact of Derrida's work for thinking about history and historiography.)

Beardsworth, Richard. *Derrida and the Political*. London and New York: Routledge, 1996. (A difficult but sharp and important account of the political dimensions of Derrida's work, especially in relation to notions of aporia and promise.)

Bennington, Geoffrey. 'Derridabase', in *Jacques Derrida*. (With Jacques Derrida.) London and Chicago: Chicago University Press, 1993. (Perhaps the best single expository account of Derrida's work, but very challenging: packed with references to other philosophical thinkers, it may not be the most immediately user-friendly for a student in literary studies.)

Bennington, Geoffrey. *Legislations: The Politics of Deconstruction*. London and New York: Verso, 1994. (This is, again, 'advanced reading': a collection of brilliant essays, including 'Deconstruction and the Philosophers (The Very Idea)'. Not all of the essays are specifically or consistently focused on Derrida's work, but they are all profoundly informed by it.)

Bennington, Geoffrey. *Interrupting Derrida*. London and New York: Routledge, 2000. (A fine but demanding series of essays concerned with 'interrupting Derrida' in an at least double sense: Derrida as the great interruptor, and Derrida's texts as calling in turn for interruptive readings. Includes the essays 'Derrida and politics', 'Derrida and ethics' and 'Circanalysis (The thing itself)'.)

Bhabha, Homi K. *The Location of Culture*. London and New York: Routledge, 1994. (A dense and difficult but influential account of postcolonialism, closely informed by Derrida's work, especially in its elaboration of notions of difference, doubling and mimicry.)

Biesta, Gert J. J. and Denise Egéa-Kuehne, eds. *Derrida & Education*. London and New York: Routledge, 2001. (A useful collection of essays concerned with issues of ethics, justice and responsibility in the context of education.)

Brannigan, John, Ruth Robbins and Julian Wolfreys, eds. *Applying: to Derrida*. London: Macmillan, 1996. (A nicely varied range of pieces 'on' Derrida, including essays in relation to television and film studies, as well as an entertaining interview with Derrida himself.)

Butler, Judith. *Excitable Speech: A Politics of the Performative*. London and New York: Routledge, 1997. (A complex and insightful deconstructive account of speech acts in relation to such topics as racism, homosexuality and the military, and censorship.)

Byrne, Eleanor and Martin McQuillan. *Deconstructing Disney*. London: Pluto, 1999. (An entertaining and often incisive account focused primarily on more recent Disney films such as *The Little Mermaid* (1989), *Beauty and the Beast* (1991), *The Lion King* (1994), *The Hunchback of Notre Dame* (1996).)

Caputo, John D. *The Prayers and Tears of Jacques Derrida: Religion without Religion*. Bloomington: Indiana University Press, 1997. (A helpful study for exploring further some of the challenges posed to religious thought by Derrida's work.)

Cardozo Law Review, special issue ('Deconstruction and the Possibility of Justice'), vol. 11 (1990), and vol. 13 (1991). (These two issues contain a wide range of valuable and insightful essays on deconstruction, law and justice. Material in the 1990 volume has also been published as *Deconstruction and the Possibility of Justice*, eds Drucilla Cornell, Michel Rosenfeld and David Gray Carlson (London and New York: Routledge, 1992).)

Castricano, Jodey. *Cryptomimesis: The Gothic and Jacques Derrida's Ghost Writing*. Montreal: McGill-Queen's University Press, 2001. (Influenced in particular by Derrida's writings on literature and psychoanalysis, an intriguing study focusing on writers such as Edgar Allan Poe, Bram Stoker and Stephen King.)

Cixous, Hélène. *Three Steps on the Ladder of Writing* trans. Sarah Cornell nd Susan Sellers. New York: Columbia University Press, 1993. lthough specifically focused on questions of fictional writing in relation to Franz Kafka, Clarice Lispector and Jean Genet, this is a passionately deconstructive book. For more on the profound, if often unstated links between Derrida and Cixous, see Derrida's 'A Silkworm of One's Own' [SOO] and Cixous's 'What is it o'clock?' [in Cixous 1998].)

Cixous, Hélène. *Stigmata: Escaping Texts*. London and New York: Routledge, 1998. (A fascinating range of deconstructive essays, including an extraordinary piece on Derrida entitled 'What is it o'clock? or The door (we never enter)'.)

Clark, Timothy. *Derrida, Heidegger, Blanchot: Sources of Derrida's Notion and Practice of Literature*. Cambridge: Cambridge University Press, 1992. (Like Bennington, Clark refers to philosophical texts a good deal so inevitably this is a challenging book for students in English Studies. Nevertheless it is written with a sharp eye for making things as clear and precise as possible for advanced students of all sorts. The Introduction and first chapter are particularly helpful.)

Clark, Timothy. *The Theory of Inspiration: Composition as a Crisis of Subjectivity in Romantic and Post-Romantic Writing*. Manchester and New York: Manchester University Press, 1997. (A compelling account of theories of inspiration richly conversant with Derrida's work. Includes a fine chapter on poetry and Derrida's 'Che cos'è la poesia?' [Che].)

Cohen, Tom, ed. *Jacques Derrida and the Humanities: A Critical Reader*. Cambridge: Cambridge University Press, 2001. (An excellent collection of essays on Derrida in relation to a variety of topics and disciplines. Includes Derrida's 'The future of the profession or the university without condition' [also in WA], Geoffrey Bennington's 'Derrida and politics', Peter Fenves's 'Derrida and history', Peggy Kamuf's 'Derrida and gender', Bernard Stiegler's 'Derrida and technology', and, especially helpful for students in literary studies, J. Hillis Miller's essay 'Derrida and literature'.)

Critchley, Simon. *The Ethics of Deconstruction: Derrida and Levinas* 2nd edn. Oxford, UK and Cambridge, US: Blackwell, 1999. (A wide-ranging and thoughtful account of deconstruction and ethics, originally published in 1992, now updated and expanded.)

Culler, Jonathan. *On Deconstruction: Theory and Criticism after Structuralism*. London: Routledge and Kegan Paul, 1983. (Among the most accessible introductory accounts of Derrida's work, partly because it takes the opposite tack from Bennington (1993), i.e. it is written very much with the literature student in mind and tends to avoid in-depth engagement with philosophical texts.)

de Man, Paul. *The Resistance to Theory*. Minneapolis: University of Minnesota Press, 1986. (This collection gives a good sense, I think, of the extraordinary deconstructive power of de Man's work. Two essays to turn to first of all might be 'The Resistance to Theory' itself, together with the brief but characteristically compact 'The Return to Philology'.)

de Vries, Hent. *Philosophy and the Turn to Religion*. Baltimore: Johns Hopkins University Press, 1999. (A difficult but excellent study of the implications and effects of Derrida's work for thinking about religion and religions.)

Düttmann, Alexander García. *At Odds with AIDS: Thinking and Talking About a Virus* trans. Peter Gilgen and Conrad Scott-Curtis. Stanford: Stanford University Press, 1996. (A powerful account of AIDS in relation to deconstructive thinking on identity and difference, death and the viral.)

Elam, Diane. *Feminism and Deconstruction: Ms. en Abyme*. London and New York: Routledge, 1993. (Engaging and important account of the co-implications of deconstruction and feminism.)

Feder, Ellen K., Mary C. Rawlinson and Emily Zakin, eds. *Derrida and Feminism: Recasting the Question of Woman*. London and New York: Routledge, 1997. (A thought-provoking collection of essays, focusing on topics such as truth, maternity, euthanasia, the innumerable and the masculine symbolic.)

Gasché, Rodolphe. *The Tain of the Mirror: Derrida and the Philosophy of Reflection*. Cambridge, MA: Harvard University Press, 1986. (A formidable and uncompromisingly 'philosophical' account of Derrida's work. Important among other things for having provided a corrective to daft notions of 'literary deconstructionism' fashionable in the 1980s, especially in the US.)

Gasché, Rodolphe. *Inventions of Difference: On Jacques Derrida*. Cambridge, MA: Harvard University Press, 1994. (A difficult but brilliant series of expository readings of Derrida's work in relation to such subjects as reason, God and the 'yes'. Includes Gasché's groundbreaking 1979 essay, 'Deconstruction as Criticism'.)

Hall, Gary. *Culture in Bits: The Monstrous Future of Theory*. New York: Continuum Books, 2002. (A lively, entertaining and often incisive deconstructive account of culture and cultural studies.)

Hobson, Marian. *Jacques Derrida: Opening Lines*. London and New York: Routledge, 1998. (More philosophical than literary in its references, this is a dense and demanding book, definitely for the more 'advanced' reader. It is a very rich and important work, nevertheless, constantly opening up new 'lines' for thinking about Derrida and the future possibilities of 'writing'.)

Holland, Nancy J., ed. *Feminist Interpretations of Jacques Derrida*. University Park, Pennsylvania: Pennsylvania University Press, 1997. (A useful collection of essays, including Gayatri Chakravorty Spivak's 'Displacement and the Discourse of Woman' and Peggy Kamuf's 'Deconstruction and Feminism: A Repetition'.)

Johnson, Christopher. *System and Writing in the Philosophy of Jacques Derrida*. Cambridge: Cambridge University Press, 1993. (A clear and engaging study, especially detailed and helpful in its account of Derrida's elaboration of a new 'concept' of writing. Includes a valuable chapter on Derrida's work in relation to evolution and the 'life' sciences.)

Johnson, Christopher. 'Derrida and Science', *Revue Internationale de Philosophie*, vol. 52, no. 205 (1998): 477–93. (A lucid and helpful exposition of Derrida's work in relation to information theory, genetic and other forms of contemporary science.)

Kamuf, Peggy. *The Division of Literature, or, The University in Deconstruction*. Chicago: Chicago University Press, 1997. (An important book concerned with the interrelations between deconstruction, literature and the institution of the university.)

Krell, David Farrell. *The Purest of Bastards: Works of Mourning, Art, and Affirmation in the Thought of Jacques Derrida*. University Park, Pennsylvania: Pennsylvania State University Press, 2000. (A lucid and impressively wide-ranging account of notions of mourning across Derrida's writings. The title of Krell's book, by the way, is taken from a self-description in one of Derrida's 'Envois' [E].)

Lacoue-Labarthe, Philippe and Jean-Luc Nancy. *Retreating the Political* ed. Simon Sparks. London and New York: Routledge, 1997. (An important collection of texts concerned with the effects of Derrida's work for thinking about politics and the political, including fascinating material on the Centre for Philosophical Research on the Political, set up in Paris in 1980. Originally published in French in 1979–83.)

Llewelyn, John. *Derrida on the Threshold of Sense*. Basingstoke: Macmillan, 1986. (A short, subtle and witty book, containing many clear and insightful comments on Derrida's work.)

McQuillan, Martin, Graeme Macdonald, Robin Purves and Stephen Thomson, eds. *Post-Theory: New Directions in Criticism*. Edinburgh: Edinburgh University Press, 1999. (A collection of essays on philosophy, psychoanalysis, literature, geography, Marxism and queer theory concerned with what the editors call the 'post-theoretical condition'.)

Miller, J. Hillis. *Speech Acts in Literature*. Stanford: Stanford University Press, 2001. (A lucid and extremely engaging book on various ways of exploring this topic, especially in relation to the work of Derrida.)

Monstrism. Oxford Literary Review, vol. 23, 2002. (Drawing on Derrida's work especially in relations to figurations of the monstrous and monstrosity, a collection of experimental essays by Andrew Bennett, Geoffrey Bennington, Timothy Clark, Peggy Kamuf, Caroline Rooney and Nicholas Royle.)

Norris, Christopher. 1997. *Against Relativism: Philosophy of Science, Deconstruction and Critical Theory*. Cambridge, MA and Oxford: Blackwell. (Helpful for thinking about some of the more 'scientific' issues and implications of Derrida's work.)

Papadakis, Andreas, Catherine Cooke and Andrew Benjamin, eds, 1989. *Deconstruction: Omnibus Volume*. London: Academy Editions. (A striking and unusual 'coffee-table book', including Derrida's 'Fifty-Two Aphorisms for a Foreword' and an extensive, splendidly illustrated ries of pieces on 'Deconstruction and Architecture'.)

tnitsky, Arkady. 1994. *Complementarity: Anti-Epistemology after Bohr Derrida*. Durham (North Carolina) and London: Duke University s. (A dense but important book concerned with exploring links een deconstruction and Niels Bohr's theories of quantum physics.)

Rand, Richard, ed. *Logomachia: The Conflict of the Faculties*. Lincoln, Nebraska, and London: University of Nebraska Press, 1992. (A good collection of essays on the implications and effects of deconstruction for thinking about the university as an institution. Includes Derrida's 'Mochlos' and 'Canons and Metonymies: An Interview with Jacques Derrida'.)

Rapaport, Herman. *Heidegger and Derrida: Reflections on Time and Language*. Lincoln, Nebraska, and London: University of Nebraska Press, 1989. (A valuable account of Heidegger and Derrida, especially interesting for its focus on such topics as ghosts and apocalypse.)

Rapaport, Herman. *Later Derrida: Reading the Recent Work*. London and New York: Routledge, 2003. (A provoking, richly informed work focusing on such topics as cultural studies, trauma, postcolonialism, the archive and existentialism.)

Readings, Bill. *The University in Ruins*. Cambridge, MA: Harvard University Press, 1996. (A polemical and brilliant deconstructive account of the contemporary university, especially in Britain and North America.)

Ronell, Avital. *Crack Wars: Literature, Addiction, Mania*. Lincoln, Nebraska, and London: University of Nebraska Press, 1992. (An incisive and wide-ranging deconstructive account of drugs, stylistically and conceptually hooked to Derrida's work, focusing on Flaubert's great novel, *Madame Bovary*.)

Rooney, Caroline. *African Literature, Animism and Politics*. London and New York: Routledge, 2000. (A fascinating deconstructive elaboration of the relations between European philosophy and African literature.)

Royle, Nicholas. *After Derrida*. Manchester: Manchester University Press, 1995. (A series of essays on deconstruction in relation to a number of different topics and disciplines including history, literature, psychoanalysis, philosophy, the visual arts and the university as an institution.)

Royle, Nicholas, ed. *Deconstructions: A User's Guide*. Basingstoke and New York: Palgrave, 2000. (Comprising work by various contributors, this is a fairly 'advanced' collection of essays. Includes Geoffrey Bennington on 'ethics', David Boothroyd on 'drugs', Timothy Clark on 'technology', Jacques Derrida's 'Et Cetera . . .' [Etc.], Maud Ellmann on 'psychoanalysis', Robert Smith on 'film', Gayatri Chakravorty Spivak on 'cultural studies' and Robert J.C. Young on 'postcolonialism'.)

Royle, Nicholas. *The Uncanny*. Manchester and New York: Manchester University Press/Routledge, 2003. (A range of essays and other short texts on psychoanalysis, literature, film and so on, focusing on the writings of Freud and Derrida.)

Smith, Robert. *Derrida and Autobiography*. Cambridge: Cambridge University Press, 1995. (A dense and difficult book which nevertheless contains fine insights and astute readings of Derrida's work in the context of autobiography.)

Smith, Joseph H. and William Kerrigan, eds. *Taking Chances: Derrida, Psychoanalysis, and Literature*. Baltimore and London: Johns Hopkins University Press, 1984. (Includes a number of engaging and informative essays, including Derrida's great essay on chance, 'My Chances' [MC].)

Sprinker, Michael, ed. *Ghostly Demarcations: A Symposium on Jacques Derrida's Specters of Marx*. London: Verso, 1999. (Contains a number of vigorous, sometimes stimulating, sometimes misguided responses to Derrida's 1993 work, *Specters of Marx*, together with Derrida's characteristically meticulous and patient response to these responses, an essay entitled 'Marx & Sons'.)

Staten, Henry. *Wittgenstein and Derrida*. Lincoln and London: University of Nebraska Press, 1984. (A clear and stimulating book, giving particular attention to phenomenology and speech act theory, and foregrounding the deconstructive character of Wittgenstein's writings.)

Weber, Samuel. *Institution and Interpretation*. Minneapolis: University of Minnesota Press, 1987. (A brilliant series of essays, some of which are not explicitly focused on Derrida's work but all of which demonstrate a sharp understanding of the implications and effects of that work. Particularly recommended are the essays entitled 'Reading and Writing Chez Derrida' and 'The Debts of Deconstruction and Other, Related Assumptions'.)

Wigley, Mark. *The Architecture of Deconstruction: Derrida's Haunt*. Cambridge, Mass.: MIT Press, 1993. (A dense but thought-provoking account of architecture, space and home in the context of Derrida's work.)

Wolfreys, Julian. *Victorian Hauntings: Spectrality, Gothic, the Uncanny and Literature*. Basingstoke: Palgrave, 2002. (Drawing in particular on Derrida's attention to ghosts and spectrality, a study focused on selected works by Charles Dickens, Alfred Tennyson, George Eliot and Thomas Hardy.)

Wood, David, ed. *Derrida: A Critical Reader*. Oxford and Cambridge, MA: Blackwell, 1992. (A useful and wide-ranging collection of essays, including Derrida's 'Passions: "An Oblique Offering"'.)

WORKS CITED

Arac, Jonathan, Wlad Godzich and Wallace Martin, eds (1983) *The Yale Critics: Deconstruction in America* (Minneapolis: University of Minnesota Press).

Austin, J.L. (1975 [1962]) *How To Do Things With Words: The William James Lectures Delivered at Harvard University in 1955*, 2nd edn, eds J.O. Urmson and Marina Sbisà (Oxford and New York: Oxford University Press).

Barthes, Roland (1977) 'The Death of the Author', in *Image Music Text*, trans. Stephen Heath (London: Fontana).

Beardsworth, Richard (1996) *Derrida and the Political* (London and New York: Routledge).

Bennington, Geoffrey (2000) 'Deconstruction is Not What You Think', in *Deconstruction: A Reader*, ed. Martin McQuillan (Edinburgh: Edinburgh University Press), 217–19.

—— (2001) 'Derrida and Politics', in *Jacques Derrida and the Humanities: A Critical Reader*, ed. Tom Cohen (Cambridge: Cambridge University Press), 193–212.

Bersani, Leo (1995) *Homos* (London and Cambridge, MA: Harvard University Press).

Blair, Tony (2001) Speech at the Labour Party Conference, Brighton, in *The Guardian*, 3 October, 4–5.

Blanchot, Maurice (1999) 'The Narrative Voice (the "he", the neuter)' [1968], in *The Station Hill Blanchot Reader: Fiction and Literary Essays*, trans. Lydia Davis *et al.* (Barrytown, New York: Station Hill), 459–69.

Bloom, Harold (1994) *The Western Canon: The Books and School of the Ages* (New York: Harcourt Brace).

Bowen, Elizabeth (1962) *The Death of the Heart* [1938] (Harmondsworth: Penguin).

Brontë, Emily (1990) *Wuthering Heights* [1847], 3rd edn, eds William M. Sale Jr and Richard J. Dunn (New York: Norton).

Brunette, Peter and David Wills (1989) *Screen/Play: Derrida and Film Theory* (Princeton, NJ: Princeton University Press).

Byrne, Eleanor and Martin McQuillan (1999) *Deconstructing Disney* (London: Pluto).

Davis, Robert Con and Ronald Schleifer, eds (1985) *Rhetoric and Form: Deconstruction at Yale* (Norman, Oklahoma: University of Oklahoma Press).

de Man, Paul (1983) *Blindness and Insight: Essays in the Rhetoric of Contemporary Criticism*, 2nd edn (originally published 1971) (London: Methuen).

—— (1989) 'Introduction to the Poetry of John Keats', in *Critical Writings 1953–1978*, ed. Lindsay Waters (Minneapolis: University of Minnesota Press), 179–97.

—— (1996) 'Sign and Symbol in Hegel's *Aesthetics*', in *Aesthetic Ideology*, l. Andrzej Warminski (Minneapolis: University of Minnesota Press), –104.

hope, Antony (1996) 'Derrida and British Film Theory', in *Applying: rrida*, eds John Brannigan, Ruth Robbins and Julian Wolfreys 'on: Macmillan), 184–94.

, E.M. (1976) *Aspects of the Novel* [1927], ed. Oliver Stallybrass 'ndsworth: Penguin).

—— (1979) *A Passage to India* [1924], ed. Oliver Stallybrass (Harmondsworth: Penguin).

Fowles, John (1999) 'Hardy and the Hag' [1977], in *Wormholes: Essays and Occasional Writings*, ed. Jan Relf (London: Vintage), 159–77.

Freud, Sigmund (1984) 'Mourning and Melancholia', *Pelican Freud Library*, vol. 11, trans. James Strachey, ed. Angela Richards (Harmondsworth: Penguin).

—— (1985) *Totem and Taboo* in *The Origins of Religion*, *Pelican Freud Library*, vol. 13, trans. James Strachey, ed. Albert Dickson (Harmondsworth: Penguin).

Gasché, Rodolphe (1999) 'A Relation Called "Literary"', in *Of Minimal Things: Studies on the Notion of Relation* (Stanford: Stanford University Press), 285–308.

Glendinning, Simon, ed. (2001) *Arguing with Derrida* (Oxford and Malden, MA: Blackwell).

Hobson, Marian (1998) *Jacques Derrida : Opening Lines* (London and New York: Routledge).

Kafka, Franz (1992) *The Complete Short Stories of Franz Kafka*, ed. Nahum N. Glatzer (London: Minerva).

—— (1994) *The Collected Aphorisms*, trans. Malcolm Pasley, Preface by Gabriel Josipovici (Syrens: London).

Kamuf, Peggy (2002) 'Introduction: Event of Resistance', in Jacques Derrida, *Without Alibi*, ed. and trans. Peggy Kamuf (Stanford: Stanford University Press), 1–27.

Kermode, Frank (1989) 'Endings, Continued', in *Languages of the Unsayable: The Play of Negativity in Literature and Literary Theory*, eds Sanford Budick and Wolfgang Iser (New York: Columbia University Press), 71–94.

Llewelyn, John (1986) *Derrida on the Threshold of Sense* (Basingstoke: Macmillan).

McQuillan, Martin, ed. (2000) *Deconstruction: A Reader* (Edinburgh: Edinburgh University Press).

Miller, J. Hillis (1982) *Fiction and Repetition: Seven English Novels* (Oxford: Basil Blackwell).

Naas, Michael (1996) 'The Time of a Detour: Jacques Derrida and the Question of the Gift', in *Derridas*, special issue of the *Oxford Literary Review*, vol. 18, eds Timothy Clark and Nicholas Royle, 67–86.

Poe, Edgar Allan (1978a) 'Preface to Marginalia', *Collected Works of Edgar Allan Poe*, vol. 3, ed. Thomas Ollive Mabbott (Cambridge, MA: Belknap Press).

—— (1978b) 'The Fall of the House of Usher', *Collected Works of Edgar Allan Poe*, vol. 2, ed. Thomas Ollive Mabbott (Cambridge, MA: Belknap Press), 397–417.

Royle, Nicholas (1995) *After Derrida* (Manchester and New York: Manchester University Press/St Martin's Press).

—— (2000) 'What is Deconstruction?', in *Deconstructions: A User's Guide*, ed. Nicholas Royle (Basingstoke and New York: Palgrave), 1–13.

—— (2003) *The Uncanny* (Manchester and New York: Manchester University Press/Routledge).

Rushdie, Salman (1991) *Imaginary Homelands: Essays and Criticism 1981–91* (London: Granta Books).

Schwartz, Hillel (1996) *The Culture of the Copy: Striking Likenesses, Unreasonable Facsimiles* (New York: Zone Books).

Shakespeare, William (1997) *The Norton Shakespeare: Based on the Oxford Edition*, eds Stephen Greenblatt, Walter Cohen, Jean E. Howard and Katherine Eisaman Maus (New York and London: W.W. Norton).

Shelley, Percy Bysshe (1970) *Poetical Works*, ed. Thomas Hutchinson, corrected by G.M. Matthews (London and New York: Oxford University Press).

Smith, Robert (2000) 'Deconstruction and Film', in *Deconstructions: A User's Guide*, ed. Nicholas Royle (Basingstoke and New York: Palgrave), 119–36.

Weber, Samuel (1987) 'Reading and Writing – *Chez* Derrida', in *Institution and Interpretation* (Minneapolis: University of Minnesota Press), 85–101.

Wills, David (1995) *Prosthesis* (Stanford: Stanford University Press).

Wu, Duncan, ed. (1998) *Romanticism: An Anthology*, 2nd edn (Oxford and Malden, MA: Blackwell).

GENERAL INDEX

parergon 15
performativity 22–3, 27–9, 42, 104, 105, 108–9, 136
phallogocentrism 122
pharmakon 14, 18, 49, 73, 77, 135, 138
phenomenology 54, 104
phonocentrism 37
Plato 18, 23, 26, 73, 85
play 32–4, 41–2, 121–2, 124, 137
Plissart, Marie-Françoise 38
Plotnitsky, Arkady 144
Poe, Edgar Allan 77, 87; *The Fall of the House of Usher* 90–2, 93
poematic 136–8, 141, 142
politics 8, 10, 21, 24, 32, 34, 63, 64, 104–5, 126–7, 153
Ponge, Francis 23, 120, 123
postcolonialism 144
poststructuralism 15
prayer 22, 116
preface 9, 16–17, 57, 143
promise 22, 27–8, 36, 38, 44–5, 91
psychoanalysis 73, 97, 104, 138–9, 154; *see also* Freud

quotation 1–2, 76, 148

Rand, Richard 144
Readings, Bill 144
reflexivity 88–9, 91–2, 95
religion 2–3, 8, 10, 32, 35–6, 75, 115–18, 126–7
Rembrandt 120
Romanticism 87
Ronell, Avital 135
Rooney, Caroline 144
Rousseau, Jean-Jacques 18, 25, 37, 47, 50–8, 87
Rushdie, Salman 45

Schwartz, Hillel 149, 150
Searle, John 147

secret, secrecy 45, 59, 93, 119–28, 138
'September 11' 3, 67, 113, 115
sexual difference 2, 144
Shakespeare, William 10, 26, 106–7, 113, 120; *Antony and Cleopatra* 38, 39–40, 43; *Hamlet* 8, 9, 109, 151; *King Lear* 113–14; *Othello* 114; *Romeo and Juliet* 23, 39–40, 122–3
Shelley, Percy Bysshe 64; *The Question* 139–42
signature 119–24
singular, singularity 10, 68, 82, 94, 99, 107–8, 119–26, 131–3, 146
Smith, Robert 150
Sollers, Philippe 86
space, spacing 14, 72, 79
speech 8, 37–8, 51–3, 64
speech act theory 21–3, 29, 144; *see also* performativity
Spivak, Gayatri Chakravorty 48, 144
Sprinker, Michael 144
Starobinski, Jean 52
Stevens, Wallace 87
Stiegler, Bernard 56, 144
supplement 14, 16–17, 18, 26, 47–59, 61, 75, 95, 96–7, 106, 138, 145, 146, 149

teaching 43, 44, 51, 105, 108, 126, 144
television 74
testimony 100–1, 133, 140
text 14, 21, 49, 61–9, 78, 138
Thurber, James 127–8
time 8–9, 40, 72, 79
Titus-Carmel, Gérard 14
tone 11, 34, 37, 43, 107
Torok, Maria 152
trace 14, 26, 49, 64–5, 67, 68, 83, 149
translation 10, 57–8, 63–4

uncanniness 10, 16, 26, 51, 73, 92, 111–12, 121, 142, 147

INDEX OF WORKS BY DERRIDA